BUILDER

of the

Spirit

GREG ALLEN

Gazelle
PRESS

ISBN 1-58169-108-4
For Worldwide Distribution
Printed in the U.S.A.

Gazelle Press
P.O. Box 91011 • Mobile, AL 36691
800-367-8203

TABLE OF CONTENTS

DEDICATION

*This book is dedicated to all those who hunger and thirst
for righteousness. I want to thank the Lord for His guidance
and persistence in this adventure.
I would also like to thank the following people:*

*My wife Cindy,
for being by my side through it all.*

*My mother Mary,
for the constant encouragement
that she gives.*

*My three daughters, Randie, Raine, and Katie,
whether you realize it or not, you have made me a better
man.*

*To Pastor Greg,
thank you for listening to what
God has to say.*

*And to all those who have made an impact on me,
whether it was in a good way or not. Thanks for
teaching me about life.*

FOREWORD

Builder of the Spirit is a book that's comprised of many different things, but its main objective is to help God's people build their lives in His image. Although it's truly one of a kind, I would best describe it as an inspirational non-fiction type book. Its pages are filled with love, laughter, and hope. It's not only filled with numerous stories, it also contains many life lessons. The main theme of the book is that we are all called to be builders of the spirit.

The book covers a wide range of individuals, subjects, and situations. It talks about childhood and adulthood.

It covers a lot of territory, but it also emphasizes throughout the pages that we must be prepared for the Lord's return.

The chapters follow the progression of new home construction, but that's not really the ultimate focus. The main focus of the book is to build spiritual integrity in the reader. The beginning of each chapter introduces the reader to a particular aspect of construction during the home building process. The remaining contents of the chapter looks at the spiritual aspect of life as it pertains to the subject.

Every chapter is filled with miraculous stories of how God has worked in my life and the lives of others I know. In the latter portions of each chapter I encourage the readers to make good choices for their lives. There is scripture planted throughout the book so the reader can see the truth behind the principles that are shared.

INTRODUCTION

During a time of intense soul searching, God told me to write this book. Many times He challenges us to step out in areas where we have never been before. I have never been much of a writer, but I have learned that if God says, "Be a writer," I say, "Show me the way, Lord!"

At the time, I told my pastor that I was not only a builder of homes, but also felt that God was calling me to be a builder of the spirit. The theme of this book is about building a home, but it is also about building lives.

My purpose in writing *Builder of the Spirit* is to help God's people. I hope and pray that this book will touch your life and help you to see that God never fails!

You may be wondering how to describe this book to your friends. To begin with, it's one of a kind. I encourage you to mark on the pages, highlight the things that speak to your heart, and even write notes in it. It's intended to stimulate your thinking. It will mean different things to different people because no two people are alike and no two people are experiencing the same circumstances.

When you describe this book to a friend, tell them how it touched your heart. There are simply too many stories contained within the pages not to touch the lives of those who read it. If you have a hard time witnessing, buy this book for people, especially relatives, because they are usually the hardest ones for us to reach. When they read it in the privacy of their homes, the Holy Spirit will begin to work on their minds and lives.

This book isn't a novel, it's non-fiction. A novel can be passed on from person to person after each one has finished reading it, but this book isn't quite like that. This book is the type that needs to be purchased for each particular individual.

It can be given as a gift because it is an excellent investment in a person's life, and after they read it, they will be well on their way to becoming a builder of the spirit themselves. I encourage people to inscribe it to the recipient with something like, "I bought you this book simply because I love you. Enjoy!"

I especially hope and pray that this book will touch your life, help you to see that God never fails and join the ranks of those who can truly be called "Builders of the Spirit!"

CHAPTER ONE

The Early Stages of Planning

God has a plan for each and every life that He brings into the world. We are all here for a reason. All of us have particular skills and talents that He can use, though some of us know what we are capable of and some do not. For instance, I did not think that I could write this book, but with God's guidance I am doing it. You can do anything if you put your heart into it.

The miracle of birth is amazing to me, but what is even more amazing is that God knows who you are and what you will be even before you are born (Jeremiah 1:5). Ask a young child what they want to be when they get older and you will hear things like doctor, fireman, policeman, or model. We all come into this world with hopes and dreams, but you never hear a child say that they want to be a drug dealer when they grow up. All children grow up wanting to become something positive, but Satan does his best to steal their hopes and dreams. But no matter what you have experienced in your life, Jesus can change your circumstances and set you free.

I came into this world on August 26, 1957 in Lebanon, Indiana. My father got my mother pregnant, and they decided to get married. That probably wasn't a good idea, but God had a plan. When my mom was pregnant with me, my dad tried to talk her into giving me to his brother because he and his wife could not conceive, but I am truly glad that Mom decided to keep me. I also thank God that she did not abort my brother or myself. I take a stand against abortion because I firmly believe it is murder.

My mother and father were together for roughly ten years. Throughout those years of marriage, Mom would pray, attend church, and cry out to the Lord for help. There were also times that Mom thought she was losing her mind, but even though it seemed to her that God was nowhere to be found, He had a plan.

God Had a Plan

One night, just when my mom felt that her faith was at the breaking point, God spoke to her. If you have lived for the Lord any length of time, you know that God is never early and He is never late. He is always right on time. This was fifteen months after my father had left us and sued her for divorce, and it was the night before her final day in court. Though she had no idea that her kids would be taken away from her and she would lose everything the very next day, Mom said that she would never forget God's words to her: "When thou goeth through the waters, I will withhold thee!" It was not until much later in life that she would understand God's meaning. (She would later realize that God was telling her that the waters in her life were about to get dark and muddy.)

My mother grew up believing that you marry for life, so it would have been very hard for her to divorce my father, but God had a plan for her. Their marriage ended when my father filed for divorce and Mom got the clothes on her back, a $60 a month check for her half of the house, and weekly visitation rights. The monthly checks stopped after four or five years, and Mom would never go back to that house again. My mother later said that, even though she had visitation rights, God told her to not go back.

I remember Mom taking my brother and me for a walk

once when I was around the age of six or seven. My grandmother was away on some missionary work in Texas, so we walked to her house, which was a mile or two away. Mom had just enough money to buy a loaf of bread and a package of bologna, so we stopped at the grocery store on the way. When we got to the house, Mom was able to get in, but all the utilities had been turned off. Mom made sandwiches for us and then lay down on the bed and tried to cry herself to sleep. I still remember rubbing her back and telling her, "Everything is going to be okay, Mommy."

Although there appeared to be no light at the end of the tunnel, God still had a plan. We may not always be aware of what He is doing, but He is constantly at work behind the scenes of our lives. Once I began to see Him as a Spirit that never sleeps, I began to understand how He could do such things. We must always remember that all things work for the good for those who love the Lord.

Back in the early 1960s Mom began attending a church in Indianapolis. This church conducted healing and deliverance services, and Mom said that she could not wait for Saturdays so she could go to them. The pastors of that church, a married couple, were real people of God, and if it were not for them, this story would probably have had a very different and probably tragic ending.

First Encounter With God's Power

I remember one Saturday evening when Mom decided to take us to church. I had a severe case of poison ivy at the time, so on the way over to the church Mom decided to give us a treat. We stopped at the local five and dime to grab a bite to eat, as we did from time to time. Afterwards, we walked over to the hobby shop to look around. You can imagine the look in our eyes when we walked into that shop! It was the next best thing to a candy store. There were some pretty high dollar items in that place, but I knew that Mom didn't have much money. I remember a small styrofoam airplane that looked like a hot dog, and I will never forget that plane or the look on Mom's face when I said, 'It's only 29 cents. Can I have it?" Her reply was, "Is that all you want?" As you may have guessed, I was having a very good evening, but it was about to get even better.

A guest missionary was visiting my mother's church that night and when it came time for the altar call, he asked if anyone wanted to be prayed for. My mom walked me down the aisle to this man who seemed to me to be a gentle giant. After I told him of my problem, he appeared to either be thinking about it, or asking God what to do about it. I will never forget what he did next. He whispered in my ear that God had said to spit on my arm. I thought that was gross, but that was what he said that God had told him. In the Bible the story is told of Jesus spitting on the dirt, making it into mud, and rubbing it on a blind man's eyes to restore his sight. I figure that if it was good enough for the blind man, it was good enough for me. The missionary spit on his fingers and rubbed them on the inside of my elbow. When I awoke the next day, the poison ivy was gone, and not even a scab remained. That would be my first encounter with God, but certainly not the last. I did not know it at the time, but God was in the early stages of planning my spiritual life. It would not be until much later that I would know that we are temples of the Holy Ghost. I realize now that He was starting to build His temple in me, and I would encourage you to find this truth for yourself in God's Word. It would be another 15 years before I would ask Jesus to come into my heart, but I never forgot that night.

Dealing With Loss

Soon came the time for my brother and me to go live with our father, and I cannot imagine the heartache my mother felt that day. At the time, I could not understand why God would tell my mom to never go back to that place again. People would ask her why she did not visit her kids when she had visitation rights, or why she did not fight for the kids. Mom said very little about these matters, because people just did not understand what God was trying to do.

On the day that my mother was leaving our house, another woman was sitting outside waiting to move in. I remember Mom's pastor paying us a visit the first week of Mom's absence. He was a small man, but he had boldness like I had never seen before. He asked where Mary was, and the woman whom Dad just happened to be living with told him that she was gone. I will never forget what that powerful man of God said. He kept saying, "This is not right. This just is not right." Before he left, he asked if my brother and I were all right. I told him that we were, but he walked away shaking his head. That woman would try to become our mother, but we would never accept her.

The court told my mother that she had to leave, but her question was, "What do I do and where do I go?" As always, God had an answer for her. She was able to live with her brother until she could afford a place of her own and God gave her a job very quickly. God was in the early stages of planning her restoration. Many times she thought that her kids would think that she had abandoned them, and they would never want to see her again. That sounds just like a thought that Satan would put into your head, doesn't it? Always remember that God is good and Satan is bad, and God always wins.

Mom's job was at Stewart Warner right across the street from our house. Stewart Warner was in the heating and cooling business, but this plant had been converted into an ammunition assembly line, producing mortar shells and fins at that time when the Vietnam War was being fought. Since the demand was great for these items, Mom got to work a lot of overtime. I was a smart little guy, and I had a perfect plan. Dad got home from work at 4:00 in the afternoon, and Mom got off work at 3:30. I can remember the first day that I decided to go pay Mom a visit at work. I remember thinking, "Boy, Mom sure will be surprised when she comes out that door!" I waited outside for her, and I must say that I was nervous. As the people started filing out of the building, I knew that my hopes of seeing her were about to become a reality. I will never forget the look on her face when she saw me. She started crying, and I ran to her and started crying myself. I told her that I loved her, and she cried some more. I also remember the faces of her fellow employees. There was not a dry eye in the crowd. One lady walked Mom home, and they both cried all the way.

Childhood Problems

Now that I had figured out a way to see Mom without Dad knowing about it, I felt a little better but was still mad at the world. I was not the perfect student. In fact, I was hell on wheels at the elementary school that I attended. I did not like school and tended to be an average student. Now that I look back on it, I had no one to blame for my actions but myself. God holds us accountable for our actions, you know. His Word says to obey the laws of the land and, though I am not proud of it, I broke the law a few times myself.

I would have to say that I had more good teachers than bad ones. I can remember one of my fourth grade teachers who, in my opinion, lacked wisdom. I will never forget her words to me: "Your life-long ambition will be to hang off the back of a garbage truck!" I'm 44 years old, and I can still remember that one. Kids need positive reinforcement, not negative. If you tell a child that they are worthless, sooner or later, they may start believing it. Keep this in mind the next time you become mad or frustrated with a child. Jesus covered this subject in Matthew 12:36. He said, "But I tell you that men will have to give account on the Day of Judgment for every careless word they have spoken."

My nineteen-year-old daughter, who attends an Indianapolis university, is planning to get her bachelor's degree in elementary education, and I have told her several times that teachers should do what they do for the love of children. She knows that she will probably not get rich from that job but feels that the impact it will make on young lives is worth it to her. A teacher typically spends more time with your children than you do during the course of the school year. Parents trust teachers with their most cherished gift, so if I were to give teachers one piece of advice, it would be to take care in what you say and do around those young minds. God is watching and so are the parents!

I always like to ask people who was their favorite teacher. Ask yourself that question. If you still know that teacher's whereabouts, give them a call or write them a note thanking them for all they did. Believe me, it won't fall on deaf ears. About a year ago, I received a call from my sixth grade teacher, wanting me to do some work on her house and I happily agreed. This dear woman of God had lost her husband a short time back, and I think she just needed someone that she could trust. In fact, I remember once when she took me to the side one day and said, "Jesus loves you, and so do I." She's in her 70s now, but she is still the kind and gentle person that I have always known, so different from my fourth grade teacher who had predicted my failure in life. One day when I was pouring cement at her house, we took a break to talk on the front porch and she told me that my fourth grade teacher had suffered a nervous breakdown that year and had taken a leave of absence. She would later be placed in a nursing home and eventually die there. When I told this customer of mine what the fourth grade teacher had said to me when I was young, she started crying. I still see my sixth grade teacher every week and try to give her a hug every chance I get.

A few months ago, my family and I were eating at a local restaurant and I saw someone that I should have apologized to years ago. The man was my fifth grade teacher, and I had placed a tack in his seat years before. I walked over to him in the restaurant and asked him to forgive me for the stupid thing that I had done 30 years before. He told me not to worry about it because that was a long time ago. It may have been a long time ago, but I still needed to ask him to forgive me.

God's Word tells us that we need to walk in love and forgiveness. When Jesus was asked how many times we should forgive our brother, His answer was seven times seventy. It is never too late to ask for forgiveness, no matter how old you are. Jesus can come into your heart and forgive you of your sins. All you have to do is ask. And don't wait until you are on your deathbed to do it. It's possible to ask Jesus to save you at the last minute, but why chance it? If God can save a prisoner on death row, he can surely save you. When we make mistakes, the only thing we have to do is ask the Lord to forgive us. God forgives us when we ask and then He throws the sin into the sea of forgetfulness! So, if God can forgive and forget, why can't we? I will give you a clue, and it's spelled P-R-I-D-E!

God hates pride and has called us, as His children, to be humble. As a child I was far from being humble. I was full of pride because I thought I was the biggest and meanest kid on the block. Now that I look back on that deranged behavior, I realize that I was accomplishing nothing. I was a wrecking ball with no plan. Some people live their entire lives with no plan. They seem to just stumble through life with little or no purpose. Thankfully, God does not give up on us, and thankfully, He had something else in mind for me.

As I said, I was no angel. In the back of my mind, I was trying to do the right thing, but I had no guidance. As an elementary school student, I was a bully. I would do things like pull the fire alarm just to watch the entire school empty. I would kick playground balls onto the school roof so I could get attention and detention. I was the only student who was fired from the milk patrol. (The milk patrol was a small group of students that delivered milk to every student who purchased it on a daily basis.) I would drink as many cartons of milk as I could before I had to deliver them and burn the empty cartons in the boiler. The principal became suspicious and eventually fired me. There was no excuse for my behavior, but there was no one at home to stop it. I was a child in need of help, but unfortunately we live in a throw away society, and many adults are quick to judge kids as no good and throw them away. This is why we should reward our children for the good grades and deeds that they accomplish. They worked hard for what they got so they should get paid for it. You work hard for the pay that you receive, and your kids feel the same way.

When I was in second grade, I did a terrible thing. It was something that I never was able to ask the person forgiveness for, and that has bothered me ever since. I was standing in the coat closet for a punishment when the fire alarm sounded. As my teacher walked by, I stuck out my leg and tripped her. She was a very heavy woman, and she broke her leg. She retired that year, but she also retired me. I am not proud of it, but I failed second grade because of that stunt. I am trying to make a point about kids who seem to be out of control. We need to take the time to listen to what is bothering them.

When I was a junior in high school, Dad moved to Kentucky. My brother got into an argument with my father one night and my brother ran out the door and hitchhiked to Indiana where Mom lived. I would follow him about an hour later. I hitchhiked to Indiana in the middle of the winter when it was about 20 below zero. I only had the clothes on my back but didn't care.

Blessings and Curses

The Lord has helped me deal with these memories. He has wiped the pain of those thoughts from my mind. I don't know how He has done it, but he has. A few years ago, the Lord told me that even though I do not think about my father, I still have to forgive him. At that precise moment, I fell to my knees and told the Lord that I forgave my father for everything that he had done. It felt like a heavy burden was lifted from my shoulders. I know it is hard to forgive people for the terrible things that they have done to you, but you must. It is not an option.

If you know of someone who abuses children, or if you yourself have abused children, please do something about it. Children are a gift from God and they need to be loved and protected. If you are a child of God, and you have repented for such actions, God will forgive you, but what He may ask you to do will be hard. Asking for forgiveness is never easy, especially from a child. God will forgive you, but the child may not. I have heard people say that young children do not remember, but that is simply not true. Kids remember more than you think, and many times the thoughts scar them for life.

As you have seen, I was a victim of abuse and became the by-product of a bad environment. But God has delivered me from those things. Satan likes to bring up the past to cloud our minds, but that's not God. He is our forgiving and loving Father!

My father has three granddaughters that he has never met and has never asked to meet them. With God's help I overcame this generational curse, and you can too. Throughout time, people and their descendents have been cursed. When you see a curse for what it is, you can change it. Ask God to open your eyes and to put a stop to the passing of that awful torch. Both good and bad things can be passed down in a family.

On the other hand, there can be generational blessings. My mother's father, Grandpa Wilcox, was a large, kind man with a big heart. Although I never met him on this earth, I am convinced that I will see him in heaven. I have been told that he would not stand for people talking about his pastor or others that were part of the church.

During the depression, Grandpa had ten mouths to feed, but little money to do so. Christmas Eve came, and there was snow on the ground. He awoke that particular morning to an awful sound coming from outside. To his amazement, a mink that had been caught in a trap was entangled in his picket fence. Grandpa was an honest man, so he set out to ask the neighbors if the trap belonged to them. He walked for miles to accomplish that task and when no one claimed the trap, he sold it and the mink's fur. He earned enough money to buy each child a candy cane and an apple. He also had enough money to buy a little red wagon for them all to share. Grandpa Wilcox was a man of God who believed in prayer, and God answered that one! Grandpa Wilcox was a builder of the spirit.

Builders

God is calling all of us to be builders of the spirit. You do not have to know anything about construction to do it. Jesus was a carpenter while He was on this earth, but His true destiny was to be a builder of the spirit. The same calling is upon my life. I'm also a builder in more ways than one.

There are different categories of builders. God is the *Father* Builder, while Jesus is the *Master* Builder. Men like Billy Graham, Benny Hinn, and Lester Summerall are pastors who are considered to be skilled builders because they have led so many to Christ. There are entry-level builders like myself who are not in the ministry, but whom God has chosen to use for His glory. Then there are part-time builders who only work when they have to. And last of all there are the wrecking balls, who do nothing but tear down. Since God has called us to be builders of the spirit, let's not tear down. Let's build up!

CHAPTER TWO

The Dream

All of us have hopes and dreams. *Webster's Dictionary* defines hope as "the feeling that what is wanted can be had or that events will turn out well. To believe, desire, or trust." A dream is defined as "an inspiration, goal, or aim." A dreamer is generally considered to be a person who has bold ideas or plans. I never viewed myself as a dreamer until God came into my life. Now, there is nothing wrong with having hopes and dreams. Even God the Father has hope in His children. Remember, greater is He who is in you than he who is in the world. Now I feel that I can do all things in Christ, and therefore I can fulfill His dreams for me. After all, if God is for me, who can be against me?

A dreamer can sometimes be considered impractical. People who never follow through on their hopes and dreams are viewed as unrealistic dreamers. They simply talk themselves out of the fullness of life by not stepping out into it. There may be a number of reasons why this happens, but I feel the main one is fear. Fear is Satan's favorite tool and he constantly tries to use it against us to prevent us from fulfilling our purposes. When he comes against us, we can tell him, "I have no spirit of fear, Satan. You lose!"

I was sitting at home one day feeling sorry for myself when God spoke to me. He said that I had a problem with faith. I answered by saying, "I don't understand, Lord." He told me that my children never worry about their next meal or the roof over their heads. They trust their parents will provide for them. He said that I should have the faith they have—the faith of a child. How simple His ways are!

Children's play is important to the development of their character, so parents should encourage them to play. It alarms me that many children do not play outside like they used to, but instead sit in front of computers or televisions for entertainment. The things that are on television and on the Internet are disturbing. Parents need to censor what their children are watching. Some programs on the television are so disgusting that I simply unplug it.

When children are growing up they play with different toys. Girls play with dollhouses, and boys play with tools. It seems as though girls are thinking about designing their dream homes, and boys are planning on how to build them. When people get older, though, they start to seriously think about homes. "Home" can mean different things to different people. "Home" to a villager in Africa might mean a grass hut while "home" to an Eskimo could mean a very large block of ice. We all need a place to lay our head, and hang our hat, but for some unfortunate individuals, "home" is a cardboard box. If you have the opportunity, visit a homeless shelter. It breaks my heart to see people that are homeless.

I strongly endorse an organization called Habitat for Humanity. founded in 1976 by a man named Millard Fuller. It is a Christian organization that provides affordable housing for those who are poor. This organization has local chapters all across the United States and accomplishes its mission by using volunteer labor and mostly donated materials. Former President Jimmy Carter and his wife are involved with this group. If you desire to be a builder of things and of the spirit, check them out. You will make new friends and become a blessing to those who are less fortunate than you. Hebrews

6:10 says that we can show God that we love Him by helping His people.

We all have dreams. Dreams of the past, the present, and certainly of the future. God would not have given us creative minds if He did not intend for us to use them, and our world would certainly lack inventions, literature, and music if it were not for creative people. God created us in His image and gave us our minds to use. He is the master of creativity, so don't be afraid to dream. Let God be creative in your life. Satan is the father of lies and will go to great lengths to convince you that you are not capable of doing anything. But God says if you have an ear to hear His Word, He will guide you and instruct you. Philippians 4:13 states that "I can do anything through him who gives me strength." Underline the word "anything!"

Encourage Dreams

From time to time, the pastor of our church will have us hold the hand of the person next to us and pray for them. A fifteen-year-old girl was standing on my left side one particular Sunday morning, and as I held her hand and prayed, I could feel the presence of the Lord upon her. When everyone was finished praying, I told her that the Lord had His hand on her, and that she would be amazed at what He was about to do in her life. After I told her this, she smiled and gave me a hug.

After the service ended, I spoke with her father. God told me to tell this man that He had His hand on his daughter. The Lord also said that her age did not matter to Him, and that what she had in mind may seem silly, but not to Him. The Lord gave this man a warning not to hold her back or he would be held accountable. The man was dumfounded. He said that he knew these words were from God because the Lord had been dealing with him all week on that very subject. The young lady had the idea of starting a Bible study group at her high school, but her father was against it. A week later, I handed her a note that read: "Follow through on your dream. God is on your side. Always remember Philippians 4:13. Good luck with your new adventure." The moral of this story is that age does not matter to God, and if you have a dream, go for it.

A new home can be the dream of a lifetime, but for some of us, it can be a very large mountain to climb. Some people never own a home and rent property for their entire lives. I understand that some individuals choose to rent because of their circumstances and that is fine, but if your desire is to be a homeowner and it feels like an uphill climb, look at what Jesus said in Luke 18:27. "What is impossible with men is possible with God." If your dream is to be a homeowner, don't give up so easily. There are many programs out there to help you with your dream.

One of my dreams has always been to share Christ with others. In the summer of 1988, I had just resigned from a job in Crawfordsville and started a new one in Lafayette, Indiana. When you serve the Lord there is a price to pay, and I paid it with that particular job. I had never been one to speak out in the work place before, but that would all change one day when a fellow employee in my department approached me. He told me that he had come very close to committing suicide the night before, and my response was. "What could be so bad that you would even think about something like that?" He said that his marriage was going under and his life was a wreck. In this case, Satan tried to paint a picture of hopelessness for the man, but thank God that he was not successful.

I said, "Do you know what you need?

He said, "What?"

I told him, "You need Jesus!"

His response was to get angry and storm out of the room, saying, "I don't know about that." A week passed, and I really prayed for this guy because I was worried about him. I will never forget the look of joy on his face one Monday morning when he told me that he and his wife had been saved the night before and Jesus had turned his thoughts and life around. You may be interested to know that this man became very successful in business, and he and his wife are very happy and living in Georgia. I still view him as a friend who was headed down the wrong path, but I thank God for using me to stand in his way.

A month later, another man in our department was experiencing similar difficulties and also gave his life to the Lord. I would like to think that I was instrumental in their conversions, but God deserves all the credit. That man became a newly reborn Christian and therefore excited about how God had changed his life, so he began telling everyone at work about his new life-changing experience. Unfortunately, my employer did not appreciate this, and it would ultimately lead to my resigning from that company. Needless to say, the remaining two weeks of my employment there were not pleasant.

I began the new job in Lafayette, hoping for a new beginning. To my astonishment, however, I walked into the same type of situation I had at the old job. I remember asking the Lord, "When will this never ending merry-go-round stop?" The Lord's response was, "I will give you your heart's desire."

Fulfillment of Dreams

My dream was to become a contractor. I had always been good at building things and had wanted to own my own business. The problem I had was that I was afraid I would fall on my face. I knew that was not God talking, and he would prove it to me.

While traveling to work one morning, I talked to the Lord about starting this new business. I told Him that if He was really going to give me my heart's desire, He would have to show me a sign so I could have peace about it. At that very moment, I hit a dove and killed it. The Lord knows that doves mean a great deal to me. They symbolize peace, and I would not kill one for anything. God reminded me that He feeds the fowl of the air and asked if I was not more important to Him than they were. I replied, "Of course Lord!" I told the Lord that if I saw another dove *after* work I would be at peace about starting a new business.

When it came time to clock out for the day, I walked out

the door and discovered that it was raining very hard. You do not normally see birds sitting out in the rain, so my first thought was that it was not God's will for me to leave that job. As I was leaving the city of Lafayette, I was thinking that God did not want me to be a contractor but suddenly was amazed at what I witnessed next. In the downpour I saw hundreds of doves sitting back to back to back on a wire between two telephone poles. I told the Lord, "That is good enough for me!" I was convinced that was a sign from God that would never be duplicated, but to my astonishment, in July of 2001 I would witness this exact same display of God's loving power again. I followed through on my dream of becoming a contractor, and I'm a much stronger person for having the courage to step out.

I love the movie "Patch Adams," which stars Robin Williams, and is based on the true-life story of a doctor who believed that laughter was the best medicine of all. He had a vision for a clinic that would treat the poor in spirit. He falls in love with a female classmate, and although she treats him cruelly he continues to show her love. After the clinic has begun, Patch's friend tells him that men have always been attracted to her. Without their saying it, you can tell that she had been raped. Patch begins to cry, and she tells him that she loves him. She says that she dreamed of being a butterfly as a young girl. They have turned into something beautiful and can fly away. The girl is later murdered, and Patch blames himself. He is thinking about leaving school and in one scene stands on a cliff thinking about suicide. He asks God why she was killed but talks himself out of jumping. As he turns around, a butterfly lands on his heart, and he begins to live his dream again. (This speaks volumes for those who have been traumatized by rape. Only other rape victims can say, "I know how you feel," but God can restore what was stolen.)

My entire family has dreams and I would like to share some of them with you. My wife Cindy is 47 years young and desires to return to college. She would like to be a writer and an artist, and it is my hope that she will allow God to use her talents. I also have three daughters. Randie has dreams of being an architect, owning a new home, and being debt free. Raine, who is 19, is focused on going to college to be a teacher. Katie, who is 15, wants just about everything. She desires to be a singer, songwriter, actress, and a registered nurse in her spare time. I am 44 years old, and I also have many dreams.

In September of 2000 I got my wish to go deep-sea fishing. My wife and I traveled to Virginia Beach, Virginia for a week's vacation. We decided to walk on the beach the Sunday evening that we arrived, and all I could do was thank God for the beautiful ocean that He created. The sounds and smells of the ocean are something that you really have to experience to appreciate.

Dreams Don't Always Turn Out

The night before we were scheduled to take a charter boat out for a day of fishing, we forgot to purchase motion sickness medicine. My wife and I met the captain and first mate early that morning and began our trip. The waves were four to six feet high, and it did not take me long to become green behind the ears. Cindy caught a small tuna, and I was happy for her but I told the first mate that I could not stand it any longer. The captain took us back to the marina and it took me about two hours to get over feeling so bad. The moral of this story is that your dreams do not always turn out like you plan.

There are also times when your dreams become shattered. In all the years that I had been in business, I had never been without work, but the first four months of 2001 were a period of utter famine. There was no work, and I was not even getting calls for estimates. However, I was not in a panic, nor was I worried. It was during this time that God told me to write this book. It's in the quiet times like these that God speaks the clearest! I had a peace that surpassed all understanding and knew that God was going to work it out. God was not punishing me but was simply teaching me to totally rely on Him. Just because we are in a valley does not mean that we will always be there. If we stop to analyze it, we will see that God is blessing us, and we don't even realize it.

I have had numerous dreams at night during the past few years. Dreams are just one of the many ways that God chooses to communicate with us. At the urging of my mother, I began documenting them in a journal. If God is using you, I encourage you to begin a journal. It is quite helpful to refer back on. I would like to share a couple of my dreams with you. One of them was set in heaven. I was surrounded by hundreds of eagles, all types—large and small. Some of these birds were soaring, some were walking, and some were perched. I was petting them, and they were rubbing their wing feathers on me. I would then discover Isaiah 40:30 & 31:

Even youths grow tired and weary, and young men stumble and fall; but those who hope in the Lord will renew their strength. They will soar on wings like eagles; they will run and not grow weary, they will walk and not be faint.

The meaning of the dream for me seemed to be that God is not only powerful, but also merciful!

I recently had a dream that I had passed away and was being shown in the local funeral home with a line of visitors backed up for miles. This dream did not mean that I was going to die, but rather that I would make an impact on numerous lives. This is my definition of success. Unfortunately, some people view material things as a guide for success. God does not care about all the money you have. He cares about what is in your heart, not in your pocket. We are all guilty of judging people by where they live or what kind of house they have. Although it is my dream to build a new home in the woods, that is not what God has entrusted me with at this time. No matter where you live, God expects you to take care of what He has entrusted you with. Maintain what you have and don't let it fall into disrepair.

If you have a dream, share it with someone. Be a part of someone else's dream! I recently purchased a 1966 Ford Mustang that my daughter Katie and I plan to restore together.

Fill your life and those of others with lasting memories. I guarantee you won't regret it.

Chapter Three

Plans, Yours or His?

Before you can start building any type of structure, your county, state or federal governing body will require that you obtain a permit. Purchasing a permit is buying permission to build. The governing jurisdiction that oversees your project has its own set of rules and regulations and the cost of a permit can range from a very small amount to thousands of dollars. Some areas of the United States have no inspectors and require no permits. On the other hand, there are certain areas in the country in which it is very difficult and expensive to obtain a permit. Building inspectors are taught that permits are a requirement for public safety. When you construct or repair a structure, there are building codes that outline the way it is to be built and the type of materials that are to be used. There is a code for everything. There are dozens of codebooks, and even one that covers the proper size nails to use. God also has a code called the code of conduct, and His codebook is called the Bible. Thankfully, you do not have to obtain a permit to build a life.

Before you can set out to build, you will need a set of plans. Before a permit is issued, the building authority will want to look at your blueprints. There are several types of blueprints and several types of plans. There are floor plans, plot plans, and elevations, just to name a few. Psalms 40:5 states that God has many things planned for us. His Word says that we are created in His image, and since we are created like him, we have a free will of our own. If you have kids, you will experience what a will can really be like! God is our heavenly Father and corrects the ones He loves but does it with a gentle hand. It is not God's will that any should perish, but since we have this thing called free will, we can choose whom to follow. You can serve the Lord, or you can serve Satan. Those who choose to serve Satan choose death and destruction. Some would say that God sends people to hell, but that simply is not the truth. They choose to serve the father of lies and are rewarded accordingly.

Through trial and error, I have gradually learned to do what God says. If you don't listen to Him, it could have grave consequences. God began to teach me about this subject about 15 years ago when I was employed at a local factory. One particular week found me working beside another employee who looked scary. God told me numerous times during the day and week to tell that man that Jesus loved him, but I failed the Lord and the man landed in jail. I told myself that it would not happen again, but ten years later I made the same mistake.

My family and I were attending a local church when my foolish reasoning would get in the way again. A young married couple was at the church that particular Sunday for the first time and God told me to tell them, "Stand like the mighty oak." I thought, *I don't even know these people* and said nothing.

Two weeks later, God told me to give them an apology and give them His word. I confessed to him that I had failed the Lord, and I had failed him and his wife. Their response was, "Why didn't you give us that word three weeks ago?" They told me that their son had rebelled against them and run away from home. The news of that made me feel even worse than I had already felt, so I walked to the car and waited for my wife to arrive. As I was dejectedly sitting there, the gentleman that I had failed walked to the car and tapped on the window. I rolled down the window, and he said, "If God tells you to tell something to someone, you better do it!"

The church that we currently attend has an excellent fireworks display on the fourth of July. In July 2001 the Lord told me to walk over to a man whom I had recently met in a church class. I do not know why, but I started talking about the spirit of indifference that our church was suffering from. Suddenly, that man looked to the sky and asked the Lord to forgive him. I have had the privilege to know this man and his family since then, and I believe him when he says that he was truly sorry. He told me that he had walked out of the market when he noticed a homeless person, and although God had told him to take that poor man home and feed him, he didn't do it and the homeless man killed himself the following evening. This shows us that not listening to what God has to say can truly have grave consequences! Talking to God is not difficult. Talk to Him like you would talk to your best friend, because He is your best friend. Paul states in Thessalonians 5:18 that "We are to give thanks in all circumstances, for this is God's will for you in Christ Jesus."

In 1995, I was driving past the church that my family and I had attended in the late 1980s. The Lord told me to turn the vehicle around and walk into that church. I told God that I was late and in a hurry, and I just did not have the time. That is not the answer He wanted to hear. I was driving a brand new pick-up truck that had a full tank of fuel, but it began to sputter and slow down. It felt like it was running out of gas and I began to realize that it was not the truck, but it was me. I turned around in the nearest driveway and headed in the opposite direction. Guess what? The truck ran fine after I turned around!

I walked into that church, and the pastor was there. I told him what God had said, but he could not accept it. He insisted that he should pray for me, and not I for him. That man would later suffer three heart attacks, but not die from them.

Folks, when someone asks to pray for you, let them!

A very similar occurrence happened two years later. I was driving down the street of a neighboring town when God decided to speak again. He told me to enter a church and speak to the pastor, but this time I would find that things were a little different. Again, I was driving a new truck with a full tank of fuel and as before, the vehicle began to sputter and slow down. It simply felt like it was running out of gas, but it wasn't. My response was, "Okay Lord, I can take a hint!" I turned around and headed in the opposite direction. When I entered that church, I found the pastor standing in the lobby. As I was talking to this man, I noticed something very peculiar. I looked down the hallway and saw what appeared to be smoke. I told the pastor that his church was on fire, but his response was, "No, it's not." I asked, "What is it?" He said that it was the Holy Spirit, that he had seen it before and to not be alarmed. The Spirit remained for only a few seconds and then it slowly disappeared. I said to the pastor, "That was the most amazing thing that I have witnessed in a long time!"

My family and I began to attend that church. We would become very comfortable with that church and its pastor, but the day would come when the Lord would change the plans. God had sent me to a church that had a pastor who was single and just needed a friend to talk to. It happened that he liked to hunt and fish, as did I. Consequently, the pastor and I became good friends. My family and I attended that church for two or three years, and we all learned and grew. God began to use me in a wonderful way like He never had before. We were getting very comfortable with our surroundings, but God was about to pull the rug out from under us.

I was sitting in a Sunday morning service when the Lord spoke to me. He simply said, "It's time to move on!" The pastor was not enthusiastic about God's new plan at all. He felt that I was turning my back on him and walking out of his life. This man, who is still just a man with human emotions, would later tell me that he had to repent for harboring bitterness in his heart. Although I rarely see or talk to that pastor, I still consider him my friend. I knew that when God said it was time to go, it was time to go!

My family and I attended no church on a regular basis for some time, and I began to think I had been hearing things before. Had the Lord really told me to leave the previous church or had it just been my imagination? There are places in the Bible that speak of patience and being still and listening. .

My wife and children began to rebel against the decision that was made. Rebellion is not something that God takes lightly. Satan rebelled, and we know what happened to him. Satan will try to get you to second-guess God, but when those thoughts come into your mind, you have to see them for the lies that they are.

God was teaching me patience. I was asking Him what to do, but He remained silent. The day finally came when I received my answer. While working on a project in a neighboring town, I made a trip to the local lumberyard. As I stood outside waiting for the assistance of the attendant, God spoke. He said, "I want you to start going to the church directly behind where you are standing." I did what God wanted and began to attend this new church that seemed larger than life. My family was still not happy, though. They missed their old church and their friends. I told them that they would meet new ones, but that was of little consolation to them. It was a relatively short period of time though before the Lord began to restore our confidence. We began to settle in and feel comfortable. We began to meet people and became friends with some of them. We are still attending that church, and God is continuing to mold us and shape us into his image. I thank Him for that!

God has great things in store for this church and its pastor. I have, on numerous occasions, told him things that the Lord has said, and he listens. He always asks, "Does it line up with the Word of God?" You should ask yourself that same question when someone gives you a word from God.

Some of us have our lives all planned out when God steps in and hands us a change order. That was the case for our oldest daughter in June of 1999. She had her life all planned out, or so she thought. She had a new car that we were paying for. She lived at home rent-free, had a very good paying part-time job, and was attending an Indianapolis university for free. She was studying to be a teacher and thought that her plans were God's, but they were not. One night her plans would crash. On one particular summer night in June, Randie and a friend were joy riding when they hit a deer. The deer was killed, and her car was totaled. When the police arrived, a report was made and the officer gave both girls a ride home. Randie would later receive word that her car was not insured at the time of the accident. She also would receive word at about the same time that her grade point average was too low, and she would have to drop out of school. On top of all that, my wife and I grounded her. The question is, did God get her attention, and did she learn her lesson? Yes He did, and yes she has. By God's grace, no one was hurt, and she was able to get her car repaired free. She now attends another college and is studying to be an architect.

When God has a plan for your life, you'd better listen to Him! In the fall of 1998 I was driving to the archery range and was slowing down on an off ramp when God said, "Forget about the archery range. Get back on the highway and drive in the opposite direction." I reluctantly did as God had instructed. The truck started to slow down when I said, "OK, Lord where am I going?" It felt like it was running out of gas. That was impossible, because it was a new vehicle plus it had a full tank of fuel. Does this sound familiar?

When the truck came to a stop, the Lord told me to walk toward the flashing red lights that were mounted on a radio tower. As I was walking through the soybean field, I was praying. I don't know what I was praying about, but God knew! As I got closer to the tower I noticed a house. It was the home of one of the board members of our church. It was a really big field, but I finally made it to the front door. I knocked, and the couple opened the door. After I had caught my breath, I told them what God had required of me. As I had been walking through the field God kept saying, "Candy-accident, Candy-accident, Candy-accident." The dad, mom, brother, and brother's girlfriend, were in shock. Candy was the name of their daughter, and she was driving back from Oklahoma. I told everyone to drop to their knees, hold hands, and pray. I don't know how long we prayed, but we prayed hard! About twenty minutes later, the phone rang. It was Candy, and she said she had just left St. Louis, which has several major interstates running through it. Something had told her to stop before she got to St. Louis. She doesn't know why she stopped, but she did. After she had taken a short break, she started driving again. Candy said that she saw no cars on the road all the way through St. Louis. If we had not prayed, it may have turned out different.

Building Relationships

Let's talk about building things. Take my advice, humble yourself and build it God's way. What I have to say now should be of great importance to you if you have grandparents that are still alive, or you have grandchildren that live close to you. They say that hind site is 20/20, and if I were able to re-draw the plan, I would have spent more time with both my grandmothers. Unfortunately we cannot rewind the tape of life. We need to seize the opportunity while we can. We need to build relationships.

In Asian cultures, parents live with their children when they become senior citizens. I have asked my mom to live with us more than once, but she is not yet ready. When she is ready for help, I will be there for her. American culture says to stick your parents in a nursing home when they become inconvenient, but do you really think that is God's will? I have visited nursing homes before, and they are heart breaking. The children place their parents there because they simply will not take the time that is required. But don't be like me. Spend as much time as you can with your grandparents and your grandchildren while the ink on the plan is still wet!

My mother lives approximately 15 miles away and her

grandchildren used to love to spend the night with her. As the kids got older, they rarely saw her because they thought they were too busy. All three girls had become teenagers, and my mother knew nothing about them. I have learned through the years that God is very organized, and that He always has a plan. God also has some great ideas if we only have an ear to hear them! What He was about to do was amazing.

God gave me a clever plan to help my mother and her three granddaughters get to know each other better. Each girl spends one entire day with her grandmother every third month. When it is that particular girl's month, she plans out the day and schedules it with her grandma. My girls were reluctant at first, but they now look forward to their month with grandma and have learned many new things. Mom and the girls have seen some neat things and traveled to some amazing places. If you are struggling with knowing someone, try God's plan. It never fails.

I have a friend who lives in a neighboring town about 30 miles away. He's the head usher at our church and, though I can't explain it, I was drawn to him like a magnet and he says he felt the same way about me. He was on the police force of his town for roughly 30 years and even held the position of police chief. He is now retired and really enjoying life!

This dear man of God that I am speaking of calls me his buddy. I consider that an honor. If someone calls you their buddy or best friend, hold that in high esteem. It is an honor to be considered someone's best friend because they are entrusting you with their friendship. It is not God's will that you have no friends. I wish I had a few more!

My friend shared an amazing story with me. Two men had robbed the local grocery store and the police gave chase. The men were eventually cornered in a nearby woods and since my friend was the chief, he was calling the shots. Something told him not to storm the woods, but to wait until morning. Morning came and God said, "Go back to the police station." When my friend gave the order to withdraw and head back to the station, you can pretty much guess what happened. His fellow officers began to rebel, and to think that he was crazy for letting those criminals get away.

Soon after their return, a phone call from a neighboring restaurant owner came in. The owner said, "Your boys are walking down the road. They are unarmed, and you can pick them up!" The police picked the criminals up and hauled them in for questioning. They were arrested for robbery and asked the officers why they had not stormed the woods. My friend said, "Something told me not to." They revealed that they had been heavily armed and could have held off an army and said, "You may have killed us, but we would have taken a lot of you with us." My friend's fellow officers were amazed that he had known God's will. The moral of this story is if you do not listen to God, it could get you killed!

I was once ticketed for an expired license plate. Although I didn't realize it was expired, it was still my fault, and the state policeman was justified to fine me. As I received the ticket, I noticed something different about this officer. He was listening to Christian music on his squad car radio and I asked him if he was a Christian. He stated that he was, and asked if I was. Of course, I said yes. He said, "Praise God! Here's your ticket and have a great day." I shook the officer's hand and thanked him for not being ashamed to tell others about his faith. Use wisdom when talking to others, but never be ashamed to tell people about your faith!

Let's talk about letting God down. Part-time employees in the body of Christ are people who want the full-time benefits without any work. It is not God's will for you to be a do nothing part-timer in the body of Christ. God has work for us, and we should be about His business. The bottom line is that God is not pleased with us sitting on our hands!

I became complacent about writing this book after chapter one. It was the first week after the chapter was complete, and I did not write for three or four days. God strongly convicted me of my laziness the following day and He told me to look up Philippians 2:3-5. It reads as follows:

Do nothing out of selfish ambition or vain conceit, but in humility consider others better than yourselves. Each of you should look not only to your own interests, but also to the interests of others. Your attitude should be the same as that of Christ Jesus.

God said that he was disappointed that I had not been writing his book. It took me until 1:30 in the morning, but I wrote five pages that night and vowed to not let God down again.

My mom has always told me to stand on the Word of God. Find a scripture that speaks to your heart and your particular problem, and stand on it. It is excellent advice to believe in the scriptures. We should all stand on Hebrews 10:7.

The purpose of this book is to do God's will and help His people and my sincere prayer for you, my friend, is in Psalms 20:4: "May he give you the desire of your heart and make all your plans succeed." We are all called to be builders, and God's divine plan should be the blueprint for your life. Seek first the Kingdom of God, and then start drawing the plan. You have a set of plans and God has a set. Which will you choose to build with?

Chapter Four

Does God Know Your Address?

There is nothing quite like having a brand new address! Some of us are proud of where we live and some are not. I once saw a house built in the shape of its owner's name. On the other hand, I have also seen homes that appear to have owners who take little or no pride in where they live. Are you proud of where you are in life, or are you ashamed? Ask yourself, *Is that where I want to live? Does God really know my address, or do I desire to remain anonymous?* For some of us, these are deep and serious questions that remain to be answered.

August of 2001 was a tragic month for both our family and friends. My wife's uncle passed away in his sleep at the age of 78. A farmer, who attended our church, died of a heart attack at the age of 47, leaving a wife and three young sons. A Christian couple, with whom we frequently do business, lost one of their sons in a traffic accident. His older brother lost control of their van, killing his brother and a friend who were both just 16 years old. The 18 year old son now faces manslaughter and drug charges.

I pray that the peace of God will rest on the hearts of these families. It is never easy to lose a loved one. I have experienced glorious joy among the living, but I have also experienced utter despair. From the day we are born, our days are numbered, but if we have the peace of God in our hearts, we should not fear death at all. On the other hand, those who do not know the Lord are terrified of dying because they fear the unknown. Those of us who know the Lord have a promise that we can hold onto—one day, we will see our heavenly Father and our loved ones who have died in Christ. I do not fear my last day. In fact, I welcome it! This chapter is dedicated to our fallen loved ones.

Lost Souls

It was a hot Indiana summer day in 2000, and I was waiting for a traffic light to turn green, when I noticed a homeless man standing at a busy Indianapolis intersection holding a sign that read, "Help me, God bless you!" That man may not have had an address, but God knew where he lived. When each car passed, the man would hand the driver a small cardboard box in hopes of getting some spare change. There were two cars ahead of mine, and the homeless man placed his box in the window of the lead car. The light turned green and the driver tried to steal the guy's money, but he held onto the box for dear life. The momentum of the car speeding away pulled him to the pavement right in front of the next car, which ran over him. The driver backed up as the man crawled to the side of the road, but she never opened her door. She just sped away!

No one seemed to care about that guy, but I circled the block and parked on the side of the road where he was standing. I walked up to him and asked him to go sit in my air-conditioned truck. It took some convincing, but he finally allowed me to help him. I could tell that he did not trust me at first. When I asked him why he was standing on the side of the road begging for money when it was 98° outside, he told me that he had suffered a broken leg at the state fair, and that the carnival people he had worked for left him behind when they departed for their next stop.

This homeless man asked me what I wanted. When I said, " I want to help you," his response was, "Why?" I told him that I loved him and that Jesus did too. I pleaded with him to let me take him to the local homeless shelter, but he refused. I asked him if he had any relatives, and he said that he had a brother who lived in Idaho. I asked him if he wanted me to drive him to Idaho, and he started laughing and said, "You're joking, right?" What he said next made me cry. He said, "You say you love me and you care about what happens to me. You know something? I believe you mean it." Soon he left my pickup and went back to the street corner, although I begged him not to go. He did promise me that he would stop begging, and I hope and pray that he did. I'm reminded of Hebrews 6:10. "How can we tell God that we love him when we fill our hearts with indifference, and look the other way?"

There are lost souls in the world who have chosen not to give Him a forwarding address. He desires to communicate with them, but they choose to remain lost. He wants them to get the message, but they simply do not want to be found. Do not expect God to seek you out. You must seek him!

Hebrews 11:6 says,

Without faith it is impossible to please God, because anyone who comes to Him must believe that He exists and that He rewards those who earnestly seek Him.

Power in God's Name

In 1981, I met my wife while we were both serving our country as sergeants in the Air Force Reserves in Germany. We were assigned to a civil engineering unit and met during our summer camp that year. We dated each other for approximately six months after we returned from Europe and eventually decided to get married.

Reservists are required to be on duty one weekend a month and one week during the year. One of those weekends would be one that Cindy and I would never forget.

We were placed in the base barracks and since we were

man and wife, we were able to stay in the same room. There was only one problem—the room only had two extremely small single beds. When it came time to hit the sack, we said goodnight to each other and fell asleep in our tiny beds. At some point during the middle of the night, Cindy woke me up, and I could tell that she was quite disturbed by a dream. It had scared her so badly that she asked if she could sleep in bed with me, and we somehow managed it.

When I asked her what the dream was about, she told me that someone or something had been driving spikes through her feet and into the floor. She said that no matter how hard she had tried, she had not been able to run away.

Since God has given me the gift of being able to interpret most dreams. I told Cindy that this meant she was about to give her heart to the Lord, and Satan couldn't stand it. At that moment, an evil spirit began to beat on the metal wall lockers in the room. I said, "Get out, in the name of Jesus, and stay out!" That vile thing went outside, and banged on the down-spout for about an hour before it left. I knew what it was, but I also knew from God's Word that Satan and his band of demons must flee when they hear the name of Jesus. The name of Jesus has power! I encourage you to find this truth in the word and use it!

In just a few weeks, Cindy would ask Jesus to come into her heart. Satan knew he was going to lose the battle for Cindy's soul and didn't like it, but the puzzling part about that whole situation was that Cindy never heard the banging. I guess she needed spiritual ears to hear it. You see, God knew Cindy's address, but unfortunately, Satan did too. Thank God that Cindy chose the Father's address. It's always a matter of choice. Which address will you choose?

Listening to God

One Friday afternoon I had called it a day. It had rained us out, and I was driving home when the Lord decided to speak. He had a job for me, but I was wet and tired, and just wanted to go home! Since I'm not God, that makes me the servant, and I should listen to what he has to say. In this case, He told me to drive to a lady's house who attended our church. That's all He said: "Drive!" I had no idea what I was to say or do when I got there.

Immediately, thoughts started going through my mind, such as, "She's a married woman, and people at the church will talk," and "I'll have a flat tire on the way," but I knew that wasn't God talking. I said, "Satan, you really don't want me to see this woman, and if I do have a flat tire, I will walk in the rain to her house!" I pulled into her driveway and walked to the front door, and she was waiting for me. There was a problem though. She told me that she had contracted a rare disorder that prevented her from coming in contact with people, and could not open the door. She called it Multiple Chemical Sensitivity—an environmental illness. She told me that her husband was away that week, and that she felt like she was all alone and going crazy. She and I both started crying. She said that she had fallen to her knees that morning and cried out to God. She said, "I asked God to send me someone to encourage me, and here you are!" Before I left, I prayed for her healing. I don't know if she was ever completely healed, but God answered *her* prayers that day. He knew her address, and He knew which servant to send. But Satan also heard her prayer. He knew her address and tried to stop me from seeing her. You might like to know that she is doing well, and only has to see her specialist once a year.

A few years ago, when I was installing a chain link fence, God spoke to me very clearly. He said, "Send the piano player at church one hundred dollars." There was only one problem with that—I didn't know the lady's name or address. The Lord told me to call the church secretary to obtain the information. I was also instructed not to give the secretary my name, but only to say that it was the Lord's will. Much to my surprise, the secretary gave me the name and address without any trouble, and God told me to place the cash in a plain envelope and mail it. Lastly, He told me to tell no one of my good deed.

When we are instructed to do such deeds in secret, we

give God the glory rather than shining the spotlight on ourselves. I hope you are beginning to see that our Lord is very
persistent, and that He cares about His children. We need to
cast all our cares upon Him, as it states in Scripture.

In the summer of 2001, my company had a painting job to
do, and our customer would become a newfound sister in
Christ. You never know what to expect from a customer on
the first day on the job, and the personality of this new customer would be quite different from the average one. She was
a spirited 82-year-old who gets around better than I do.

We usually talk to our customers for a few minutes before
we start each day, and this day was no different. As Randie
and I were talking to our new customer, I brought up the subject of writing this book. When I told her that it was an inspirational book about building lives, she began to speak what
was on her heart. The longer the woman spoke, the harder
Randie began to cry. She proceeded to tell us about how she
had met her husband of 55 years. He had recently changed
his address and was residing with the heavenly Father. She
spoke of her younger years when she had been very attractive
and could have had just about any man she wanted. She said
that she had almost married someone else just before she met
her husband but had no peace about it and called the wedding
off.

God had even known her address in the 1940s. She told us
of her days as an air traffic controller in Nebraska during
World War II, when a chapter of her life would be written by a
B-17 bomber and its crew, en route from the Philippines. She
gave the pilot of the B-17 permission to land on a specific
runway. The pilot landed the aircraft but not according to her
instructions. It was, as she put it, a "hotdog stunt!" Needless
to say, she was pretty upset and decided to walk down to the
flight desk and give the pilot an earful. When she arrived at
the desk, she saw a crew member standing there and asked,
"Are you the pilot?" His response was, "No, I'm the co-pilot."
After she finished yelling at him, he smiled, and asked if she
wanted to get a cup of coffee. Still hot under the collar, she

said, "I have to work all night!" Her boss was about to write a chapter in her life, too, when he decided to let the two of them spend time together. He yelled, "You can take off early!" She reluctantly took the co-pilot up on his offer, and they walked to the top of the tower and talked all night. As our friend put it, "He flew into my life!" He was a Christian man who gave her many wonderful years.

As you may have guessed, Randie was really crying by this time. Our new friend told her, "Be patient, God will bring you the right one." If you are still waiting for Mr. or Mrs. Right, and are losing patience, remember this principle. Romans 8:27 says, "He who searches our hearts knows the mind of the Spirit, because the Spirit intercedes for the saints in accordance with God's will." If you pray, and wait on the Lord to bring the two of you together, it will truly be a match made in heaven. God doesn't want you to make a mistake, but you might if you get ahead of Him. If you think love is about sex, you're wrong. Love is all about having a lifelong friend and caring for someone more than yourself.

I truly believe that Randie sees confession as being good for the soul. Her latest confession eased her conscience but gave me the shock of my life. Recently, she told me that she had been smoking a half pack of cigarettes per day for the previous three years. Her sisters knew that she had been smoking but had never told us. Her mother suspected that she had been smoking but had convinced herself that the smell of smoke on her clothes was from her friends. As for me, I didn't have a clue. Now, as you may have guessed, we were disappointed, but we appreciated her honesty and were really glad that she had decided to quit. As parents, you can only teach your kids in the ways of the Lord and hope that they will not stray from them. But remember one thing—they also have a free will. I know it's hard, but you have to let them go. And don't worry, because God knows their address.

As this chapter winds down, I would like to give you something to think about. Make sure God knows your address, and that you know His. "The man who loves God is known by

God" (1 Corinthians 8:3). Be ready and get your life right with the Lord. When it becomes time to pass off this tired body, I will be ready for a new address. I pray that it will read something like this. #1 Main Street, Heaven, the Universe, Zip Code #3.

September 11, 2001 is a day that all of us will remember. Just as the Roman Empire once did, we too felt like we were invincible. When I began writing this chapter, I felt led to dedicate it to fallen loved ones but had no idea that the events in New York and Washington D.C. would occur before I finished it. Now, with all my heart, I dedicate this chapter to all those who died.

The images of planes crashing into buildings and of buildings collapsing will haunt our memories for quite some time. It is beyond our comprehension to think that individuals overseas could celebrate the deaths of innocent men and women. The images of people shooting guns, cheering in the streets, and passing out candy in celebration is hard to understand.

Many are comparing that attack to Pearl Harbor, but when Japan bombed Pearl Harbor, it was through a military force and on a military target. Those terrorists were twisted individuals who had a death wish, and they did what they did in the name of Allah. Don't get me wrong; I have nothing against the people of the Middle East. They are God's children and He loves them just as much as He loves us.

Terrorists kill themselves and try to take as many with them as they can, thinking that they will be rewarded in heaven. First of all, that's not how God thinks. Intentionally killing yourself will send your soul to hell. You are not only taking God's will for your life out of His hands, but you are also breaking His law.

I pose this question to you. Is your God a God of hate and destruction, or is He a God of love and mercy? Through the ages, Satan has been all about hate, death, and destruction. "He masquerades himself as being an angel of light" (2 Corinthians 11:14). He viewed himself as an equal to God, and that's why he was removed from heaven. The bible says he fell to earth like a bolt of lightning. Diligently search your heart, and ask yourself what's in there? Whom do you serve? Do you serve a God of hate or a God of love?

As I drove home that evening, I saw panic in the hearts of Americans. Every gas station I passed had lines backed up for blocks. There were dozens of complaints across the state about station owners raising the price of fuel to as much as $5 a gallon. On the other hand, many churches opened their doors for prayer, and volunteers gave blood in record numbers. It goes to show you that our true selves come out in times of crisis. What's in your spirit? When God comes looking for you, will you throw open the door to Him?

CHAPTER FIVE

What Is Your Foundation?

With any building project there are certain requirements that must be met before construction can begin. The four previous chapters pertained to pre-construction matters, but now the fun begins because we have a new agenda. It's time to start building!

The most important feature of your home is the foundation. I can't over-emphasize how important a solid foundation is. Throughout history, foundations have consisted of various materials, and it's not unusual to find older homes with foundations made of brick, fieldstone, or even logs. The most popular choice for foundations in the United States today is either poured concrete walls or concrete block. Some builders have resorted to using a treated wood framing for their foundations, but I don't recommend them. (Remember the old saying, "Cheaper is not better.")

It is standard practice to dig to a depth of about three feet in the ground for footer placement in new home construction. Footers are the concrete base that the foundation walls rest on, and they usually consist of poured concrete 16–24 inches wide, and 8–12 inches deep. A foundation actually consists of the footers and the foundation walls that rest on top of them.

Believe it or not, Jesus had a lot to say about foundations. He said,

Everyone who hears my words and puts them into practice is like a wise man who builds his house on the rock. The rain will come, the streams will rise, and the winds will blow and beat the house; but it will not fall, because its foundation is on the rock. Everyone who hears my words and does not put them into practice is like a foolish man who builds his house on the sand. The rain will come, the streams will rise, and the winds will blow and beat the house, and it will fall with a great crash" (Matthew 7:24-27).

What's your personal foundation like? As the title of this chapter asks, upon what are you building? Paul makes it very clear in Ephesians 2:19-20 that we are members of God's household, built on the foundation of the apostles and prophets, with Jesus himself as the chief cornerstone.

Webster's dictionary defines "cornerstone" as the stone representing the nominal starting place in the construction of a building, and also as something that is essential or basic. Take a hard look at yourself. Is Jesus an essential part of your foundation? If He's not, you're in trouble. Jesus is everything in my life, and if He isn't the same to you by now, I pray that He will be before you finish reading this book.

A few years ago, my family and I visited St. Louis, Missouri, which is a wonderful place, that I always enjoy visiting. It's called the "Gateway to the Midwest." Shortly after our visit that year, the residents along the Mississippi River experienced terrible flooding, and some even called it "the great flood," although I would not go that far. (There was only one man of God who experienced the true great flood and lived to talk about it, and that was Noah.) I will never forget watching the news and seeing houses floating down the river. The Mississippi River is always a powerful force, but even more dangerous when it is above flood stage.

Eventually the waters receded and the rebuilding process began. During the flood, conventionally built homes had floated right off their foundations during high water, but a local contractor had developed an ingenious design, consisting of a two-story home resting on metal I-beams. The first story was the garage, which had a sheet metal skirting that wrapped around the I-beams. The skirting was designed to break away during flooding and to allow the water to pass through the garage area. The house could withstand the pressure of the water because the metal I-beams were driven into the ground until they hit bedrock. This was an excellent idea that minimized property loss for those people who owned homes built on this design.

Virtually all steel high-rise buildings have metal I-beams that are driven into the ground until they hit bedrock, and which serve as the building's foundation. This same design is used for bridges and all large structures that must support large amounts of weight. For example, the stainless steel arch in St. Louis is an engineering marvel that weighs as much as a battleship. Engineers calculated the bedrock to be 60 feet deep so the arch has two huge concrete footers that deep.

Let's look at what we've learned thus far. A solid foundation is crucial for success, and it's essential that a structure rests on bedrock if it has a large amount of weight. But the most important lesson that we have learned is that Jesus is the cornerstone of our faith, and He is the rock on which our lives are built. He's our support and our foundation.

Before we construct a foundation, we have to cut down the weeds. God cuts us sometimes, and if you study the Bible, you will find that God's Word is sometimes called a double-edged sword. I appreciate what Jesus had to say in John 15:5,6:

> *I am the vine, you are the branches. If a man remains in me and I in him, he will bear much fruit; apart from me you can do nothing. If anyone does not remain in me, he is like a branch that is thrown away*

*and withers; such branches are picked up, thrown
into the fire and burned.*

The moral of this story is not to be a weed or a dead
branch.

Now that we've discussed foundations and footers, and
you have a general understanding of what they are, let's relate
them to your relationship with the Lord. The footers in your
life should be deep in Christ, because if they aren't, your life
will be unstable. If you structure your life on the Word of God
and long to be like Jesus, nothing will be able to crack your
foundation.

Customers call me from time to time with serious concerns about cracked foundations. When a foundation cracks,
settles, shifts, and eventually becomes uneven, it becomes a
serious structural problem. Some house foundations develop
severe settling over time, which is usually caused by poor soil
conditions or excess weight at the stress points. The foundation doesn't fail by itself, but it has help from other sources
that put pressure on it. What is putting pressure on your foundation? Don't live with spiritual defects. Eliminate the
problem before total collapse occurs.

If you have poor "soil conditions" or shifting in your life,
you will eventually have internal damage. In other words, ungodly situations in your life will cause your spiritual foundation to shift in a negative way, and most certainly cause
damage to your spirit. But remember, damaged foundations
can be fixed. I happen to know a master carpenter who does
excellent work at straightening damaged foundations.

God knows all about fixing damaged foundations.
2 Timothy 2:19 states,

*God's solid foundation stands firm, sealed with this
inscription: "The Lord knows those who are his, and
everyone who confesses the name of the Lord must
turn away from wickedness."*

Inspect your footers. Is your life level? We should all strive for a level spiritual foundation.

Persecution

From time to time, I receive calls from customers concerned about their brick flaking off. Do your friends, relatives, or co-workers view you as a "flake" because of your spiritual beliefs? Well, I've got news for you. It's called persecution, and you should expect it. Paul talks in great length about persecution in the New Testament.

All over the world, Christians are being persecuted because of their faith, and some have paid the ultimate price of losing their lives in the service of the Lord. If you read God's Word, you will find that persecution and death were experienced by many of God's children, including Jesus Himself. As a child of God, what makes you think that you should be any different?

Being a Christian is no game. You just don't turn it off and on when you feel like it. We may think that we are experiencing difficulties, but most of us will never face what the martyrs have faced. Let me ask you this: Will persecution crack your foundation, or will you stand strong no matter what may come against you? As long as Satan is around, you're in for a fight, so my advice is to get the gloves on, be ready, and put the whole armor of God on.

Jesus told Peter in Matthew 16:18, "You are Peter, and on this rock I will build my church, and the gates of hell will not overcome it." Webster's dictionary defines "rock" as a firm foundation or support. We are the church, and hell cannot overtake us.

Our society is quick to tear buildings down, even when there is nothing wrong with them. Often, they are simply removed to make room for a bigger and better structure. Buildings should not be torn down if they still have good foundations. Along these same lines, we can say that not all people are bad. Some of God's children have foundations that can be repaired. He loves all of them and sees potential in all of their lives.

A popular attitude in American society today is "Let's get even," but that's not God's plan. If love and forgiveness is a problem for you, God can remodel that part of your spiritual foundation. It is a requirement of Christian living that we love all people. I know that it may be hard to forgive someone for the wrongs that they have committed against you, but God says that forgiveness is not an option. Galatians 6:10 states, "Therefore, as we have opportunity, let us do good to all people, especially to those who belong to the family of believers."

Using Our Potential

There is a great consumer demand for remodeling today. In fact, it's a multi-billion dollar industry because many people see potential in their older home and have no desire to tear it down. Thankfully, God sees potential in us, and rather than tearing us down, He chooses to remodel us instead. Webster's dictionary defines "remodel" as restructure. If Satan has convinced you that you are beyond repair, just remember that God has a Son who is an expert at remodeling the heart. Jesus can restore you free of charge, and all you have to do is ask. What does the Lord need to remodel in you today?

At one time, my wife's favorite television show was "Home Improvement." She said that I acted just like the main character, Tim Allen, but I know that can't be true since I don't have a neighbor with a fence. Tim Allen's career has not always flourished, however. He came from a troubled childhood and was arrested for drug possession when he was in his 20s. He served 14 months in prison, but I have to give Tim credit because he did not build on a life of crime. Crime is sin, and it is a poor foundation upon which to build a life.

Some spouses build all their hopes and dreams on their mate's foundation and become totally reliant upon them. But when failure comes, which it does sometimes, they feel betrayed and lost. Products fail, men fail, women fail, children fail, and even your parents fail. All things will fail over time, but your heavenly Father will never fail you. You have a lifetime extended warranty, if you choose to receive it. It's called God's promise of eternal life through His Son Jesus Christ. Look to the Lord, rather than people, for your spiritual foundation strength.

As a boy growing up in the 1950s, I had several neighbors. I remember one particular neighbor that seemed like a regular guy, but in March 2001 the truth about that man's life was revealed. He was on the verge of death, and his conscience was bothering him. Red was a man that had built his entire life on a lie. Now in his 80s, he thought he had gotten away with it, but his conscience was telling him that he would face judgment upon his death.

Shortly before his death, Red drove to the local police station to ease his conscience and handed over a bag full of money that had been buried in his backyard since the 1940s. Most of the bills were badly damaged, but they totaled more than $200,000. For the first time, the soft spoken, mild mannered man that I knew from childhood was about to tell his deep, dark secret to the police.

The 1940s were trying times for most Americans, and Red was no exception. As a young man in his 20s, Red became desperate and made a regrettable decision. He told the authorities that he had robbed several banks in the Ft. Wayne, Indiana area at that time but had never tried to spend the money because he lived in fear of being caught. Red died before the police could finish their investigation, but an article in the newspaper said that there were indeed two, or possibly even three, banks robbed in the area on the dates that Red had described. There was no way to track the serial numbers of the bills because they were so badly damaged. God's Word says to walk in the truth, so please don't make the same mistake that Red made. Build your life on the truth.

People who claim to be Christians, but no longer walk in the truth are only fooling themselves. I have watched many who claim to be saved and born again who still drink, curse, steal, and simply live like the world does. If that's not living a lie, I don't know what is. There is no gray area of truth. Either you build on a foundation of truth, or you build on a foundation of lies. If you are truly born again, and the Holy Spirit lives within you, curse words should not be in you in the first place. Ephesians 4:29 says, "Do not let any unwholesome talk come out of your mouths, but only what is helpful for building others up according to their needs, that may benefit those who listen." I ask those who will listen: "Will you listen to the truth, or continue to live a lie?"

I would like to tell you a humorous story about something that happened to me. It was humorous at the time, but now that I have time to reflect back on it, it seems to be a true reflection of today's Church. During the course of one particular day, our area had experienced severe storms, and a gentleman called our office because he had experienced damage to his home. He needed an estimate for the damage so he could turn in a claim to his insurance company.

It was late in the evening when I arrived at his home. I knocked on the door and heard a voice say, "Come on in!" I found the man sitting in his recliner with his eyes glued to the television set. He never took his eyes off the screen but simply pointed his finger at the living room. I walked into the living room and, much to my surprise, I saw a large tree limb sticking through the ceiling. On top of all that, rain was flowing down the branches onto the floor. It seemed that this gentleman was more interested in Monday Night Football than he was his house. I wrote the estimate up and handed it to him, but we never got the job, and I never saw him again.

This story is quite similar to the story of today's Church. We are so occupied with the things of this world that we can't see the truth that stands in front of us. We are the Church, and our time is short. Jesus is preparing to return for us soon, but much like the man in the story, the house is leaking, and we have our eyes glued on the T.V. It's time for us to wake up and see the truth. If we build on the things of this world, we will be disappointed, but if we build on the foundation of truth, it will never fail us.

Whoever coined the phrase, "Sticks and stones may break

my bones, but words can never harm me," had no idea what they were talking about. Words are powerful, and they can kill. For example, remember the tragedy that occurred at Columbine High School in Colorado a few years ago? Those two young men were building on a foundation of hate because they were constantly ridiculed by their classmates. They finally acted on their thoughts, and the end result was disaster. Adolph Hitler is another example of an individual who built on the foundation of hate.

I highly recommend that you read the book, *She Said Yes.* It is the story of a brave young lady who died serving her Lord at Columbine High School. She would not deny the Lord, and it cost her dearly. She paid for her service of the Lord with her life.

Believe it or not, I had never been in a bookstore until I began writing this book. I always thought that reading was boring. My first trip was to Barnes and Noble. I discovered a whole new world and found that God was unfolding His planned journey for my life before my eyes. Now I'm hooked! You might say that I had been building on the foundation of a closed mind.

1 Thessalonians 5:11 says for us to encourage one another and to build each other up. I'm trying to build my kids up, not tear them down. Psalms 127:1 says, "Unless the Lord builds the house, its builders labor in vain." The same verse says that unless the Lord watches over the city, the watchmen stand guard in vain. What are you watching? Are you watching the Lord work in your kids' lives, or are you watching the things of this world consume them? Parents, this is the bottom line. What you allow in your child's life is your choice. After a certain age they are on their own and can make their own choices, so we, as parents, should think and choose well while they are under our care.

I will end this chapter with a quote from my daughter Katie. She says, "Your spirit is like the foundation of a house; the house is built on a strong foundation. If the foundation is a weak one, the whole house will cave in. Jesus is also the foundation of your spirit. Without Him, it will cave in." Katie told me this before I ever started writing this book, and I thought it such a revelation that I asked her to write it down for me. Katie, you are so right! God's Word says that if we raise our children in the ways of the Lord, they won't depart from them.

God is moving in a mighty way at Katie's high school, although that is not the case in some high schools across the country. My sincere hope and prayer is that God will use the tragedy of September 11, 2001 to shake the spiritual foundation of all our high schools in America. Kids, teachers, principals, superintendents, and even the school board can and will make a difference if they only allow the Lord to visit their school. If you don't think you can make a difference in your school, you're wrong! God can move mountains if you only believe and pray.

Kids, pray for your teachers and your principal. They have some rather large shoes to fill, and they will have to answer to God for your spiritual well being. If the Lord is welcome, He will move in a mighty way. The choice is yours.

When you walk into Katie's school, you see written scriptures from the Bible on the walls of the hallways, and some students even have them hanging on their lockers. Katie says that it has been that way for as long as she can remember.

Another great thing that happens each year is called, "See you at the pole," which is a short prayer meeting held around the flagpole before school starts. It's a prayer service that is attended by teachers and students alike, and I have read in the newspaper that other schools across the country are doing the same thing.

Recently, Katie's school allowed two hours for prayer and for a Christian band to play in the auditorium on the National Day of Prayer. According to Katie, the school has no plans to stop their activities on the National Day of Prayer, or end "See you at the pole." Now you can see why God is blessing her school!

Satan desires that the politicians remove God from the

schools, but God has a plan. In spite of what Satan may try, the gates of hell will not prevail. Those who pour their hearts out to the Lord at Katie's school are not a bunch of religious nuts. They are God's children, and He has them right in the palm of His hand. Pray for our schools, America. They need it!

Chapter Six

Timetable

This chapter deals with the time demands that are placed on our lives and will ask the question, "How will you use the time that you have been given?" It is my humble prayer that you will see that God's timing is everything.

Have you ever thought about how Jesus used His time? Do you think that He wasted it? That's hard to imagine. Jesus is not only a master builder, but He is also a master planner, so I'm sure He had a plan for every year, day, minute and second that He was on this earth. Time is a precious commodity, and I hope to show you the importance of your time on this earth. I also want to show you that God is truly concerned about how you use it.

The main schedule that I use in new home construction is one called a "draw schedule." This is a payment plan and work schedule all rolled up in one for the homeowner and is required by most lending institutions. It typically consists of five draws (payments) of 20%. A schedule outlines the work that needs to be done, and each successive draw is paid when a determined amount of work has been completed.

On different occasions, God talks to me in my sleep. In these instances, although I'm not dreaming, I can clearly hear

His voice in my sleep. What an honor it was for me on October 11, 2001 to hear what God had to tell me. He said: "Today is the one month anniversary of the terrorist attack on America. The citizens of the United States are living in fear. What Satan meant for destruction, I will turn into glory." He then broke down the letters in the word "HELL," and re-arranged them to mean something else: H-eaven is the E-ternal resting place for those who L-ove the L-ord.

Do you remember a song from the 1960s called, "Turn, Turn, Turn?" A group called the Byrds, who had chosen the wisdom of the Bible for their song lyrics, performed the song. Ecclesiastes 3:1-8 reads like this:

> *There is a time for everything, and a season for every activity under heaven: A time to be born and a time to die. A time to plant and a time to uproot. A time to kill and a time to heal. A time to tear down and a time to build. A time to weep and a time to laugh. A time to mourn and a time to dance. A time to scatter stones and a time to gather them. A time to embrace and a time to refrain. A time to search and a time to give up. A time to keep and a time to throw away. A time to tear and a time to mend. A time to be silent and a time to speak. A time to love and a time to hate. A time for war and a time for peace.*

My family and I have satellite television at home, and one of the channels we have is the PAX network. Recently, I was watching a program called, "It's A Miracle!" The episode that I was watching that day focused on a story of a little girl and her father, who was a policeman. As he always did, he gave his little girl a hug and kiss before he left for work, but that day would be one that he would never forget.

The girl told her father that two angels had visited her room that morning, and that they had told her to tell her daddy to wear his bulletproof vest. The father laughed when his child told him of her experience, but she repeatedly begged him to wear the vest. After he saw that she would not give up, he eventually promised to wear it. He didn't realize it, but God was about to spare his life.

The officer and his partner had a normal day until a call came for a domestic disturbance. Police officers have told me that domestic disturbances are unpredictable and can be very dangerous. When the officers arrived at the home, they knocked on the door, and a voice from inside said, "Come on in." As they attempted to open the door, a shotgun blast came through the door and hit the little girl's father. His partner wrestled the shooter to the ground and handcuffed him. The fallen officer was rushed to the hospital, where he survived. The mother recalled the response of her little girl when she told her of her father's injuries. The girl said, "The angels saved daddy's life." You'll be glad to know that the police officer is doing fine because of listening to his daughter, and that the man who shot him will be in prison for quite some time. That story is another classic example of how God's timing is everything!

Let's talk about another miracle. A young man at our church is a literal walking miracle today, and his story is a true testimony to the fact that we all must be ready. We never know when it will be our time, and God will call us out to go home.

A day that appeared to be a normal one for our Christian friend and his family turned out to be far different. Our brother had a blood vessel burst in his brain, and he was rushed to the hospital and placed in ICU. Our church flooded his room with a constant stream of prayer warriors. After a few days, the doctors gave up hope and told the man's wife to call our pastor. The doctors were ready to pull the plug on the machine that was keeping their patient alive.

Our pastor soon arrived at the hospital. I will never forget what he told me happened next. "I grabbed his hand and began to pray for the Father to welcome him home, and the next thing I knew he was squeezing my hand. It scared me so badly that I ran from the room and told the doctor, 'He's alive,

He's alive!'" The pastor said that the doctor went back into the room and said, "We're not pulling the plug on anything."

The time came for our Christian brother to go home, and he didn't remain absent from church for very long. I remember our pastor rolling the man's wheelchair to the front of the church and saying, "This guy is a miracle! He was 5 minutes away from being unplugged!" I see our Christian friend every Sunday now, and he is doing much better. He still uses a wheelchair, but he can stand for short periods of time.

This story is another clear example that God's timing is not always the same as ours. We are quick to give up, but He never quits and He never fails. Like a runner who grows weary from a challenge, they simply fall by the wayside. It's our mission to help the less fortunate. Help those who fall and don't use them to pave your own path.

Before we judge others for the hate in their hearts, we'd better take a hard look at ourselves. How many of you were overcome by anger and hate on September 11, 2001? Anger is understandable, but hatred for others is not. 1 Peter 4:17-18 tells us this: "For it is time for judgment to begin with the family of God; and if it begins with us, what will the outcome be for those who do not obey the gospel of God? And, if it is hard for the righteous to be saved, what will become of the ungodly and the sinner?" Those among us without sin should cast the first stone. I just dropped my rock, how about you?

I was told once that if Satan bothers you, you are in good shape, but if he leaves you alone, you'd better watch out. I have a brother-in-law who recently gave his heart to the Lord, and his wife gave her heart to the Lord along with him. It didn't take Satan very long to attack him, and he began to suffer health problems. Since he is a military vet, he made a trip to the VA hospital, and the doctors told him that he was suffering from depression and prescribed medication for him. My brother-in-law said that he was having nightmares from his days in the military. I told him that Satan was tormenting him, and God's children should not be depressed. Drugs are not the automatic answer. Satan and his band of demons have no authority over the children of God; so cast that nasty and awful spirit of depression off. Simply say, "I cast that spirit of depression off me. In the name of Jesus, be gone!" If you truly believe the Lord will get that cruel and dark monkey off your back, Psalms 9:9 will give you hope. "The Lord is a refuge for the oppressed, a stronghold in times of trouble." A Christian should never live with depression. That's the time to call on God for protection.

People often say, "Boy, that sure was lousy timing." Well, in 1992, my clock was set back a bit. We were building a new home one week before the departure date for our vacation, and I was working on a platform 20 feet in the air when it collapsed. I fell to the floor and broke both feet. The theme park and hotel tickets that we had purchased in advance were non-refundable, so we didn't have any choice but to go. Now, you might think that was a bad thing, but as it turned out, handicapped people in wheelchairs get to go to the front of the lines at Disney World. We left for Florida, spent two weeks there and had a great time together as a family.

After I got back from vacation, it came time to remove the casts from my feet. I remember asking the doctor when I could go back to work. He said, "Tomorrow," and I recall going to work on that Friday and feeling lousy. I returned home around 4:00 P.M., and suddenly it hit me. I felt like I was having a heart attack. I drove myself to the hospital where they diagnosed me with pneumonia. The doctors gave me a week's supply of antibiotics and pain pills. The pills didn't seem to help much, and I ran out of them by the end of the week. I had a problem, though. The prescription had no refills.

I told my wife to drive me to another hospital, because I knew there was something terribly wrong with me. I went to the emergency room and was checked out by one of the hospital doctors. He also told me that I had pneumonia, gave me a prescription, and told me to go home.

By that time I was getting a little hot under the collar. I told the doctor that I knew I had pneumonia and that the pills the other doctor had given me hadn't worked. I told him that something was drastically wrong with me. I said, "I have been experiencing what feels like heart attacks every few hours, all week. I try to sleep sitting up because when I lay down, I can't breathe. I want you to admit me so we can find the problem before it's too late!" That didn't go over very well with him. He said, "If we can't justify admitting you, the insurance company won't pay for it!"

I said, " I have insurance!"

The doctor said, "I know, but that doesn't mean they will pay."

I told the doctor to call my physician and get his permission to admit me, and that he and I would talk about it tomorrow. The doctor left the room, but came back a short time later and said that my physician was on vacation and couldn't be reached. I asked, "Who's filling in for him?" The doctor told me, and I said, "Let's get his permission."

The doctor once again left the room and came back a short time later. He said, "We're going to do a day-stay."

I asked, "What's that?"

He answered, "If we can't figure out what is wrong with you, we have to send you home tomorrow." I remember saying, "Thank God."

The next morning came, and the doctor on-call paid me a visit. Once again, he told me that I had pneumonia, and he was sending me home. I remember looking at the clock on the wall and telling him to wait for five minutes. I said, "They'll be back."

"What will be back in five minutes?" he asked.

I said, " The attacks!"

It didn't take long for the attacks to begin. I screamed bloody murder, and it scared the doctor so badly that he threw his clipboard down and ran from the room. He returned with two nurses and ordered them to shoot me up with a painkiller. After I settled back down, he placed his hand on my shoulder and said that he was sorry for doubting me. I will never forget what he told me next. He said that he had been in the hospital once and been having a heart attack, but no one had believed him. He said that he had almost died.

The next question that came from his mouth next not only surprised me, but made me cry. He asked, "Do you know Jesus Christ as your personal Lord and Savior?"

I said, "Yes, and I really appreciate you asking me that."

Before the doctor left, he said, "You're not going anywhere until we get to the bottom of this!"

I lay in that hospital bed for the next four days and my physician, who was now back from vacation, would stick his head in the door every day and ask me how I felt. I always said, "Lousy!" After four days of that, I got tired of lying there with no answers, so I told my physician to get a second opinion or I was going to fire him.

He said, "You can't fire me."

I said, "If I don't pay you, your fired."

That made him mad. Before he slammed the door, he said, "I guess we'll have to get a second opinion."

I said, "Thank you. It's about time!"

I was visited by a lung specialist a few hours later, and he told me that when my feet had been removed from the casts, blood clots had developed, broken loose, and traveled to my right lung. Those clots killed the bottom tip of my right lung, and I would never again have the same lung capacity. He told me that I was a very lucky man. If those blood clots had gone to my heart or brain, I would not be here to talk about it. God was telling me, "Greg, it's not your time. I have work for you to do."

Around the first of the year, I knew in my spirit that God wanted me to do something, but I just didn't know what it was. I tried to get involved with just about everything I could at church, but none of it worked. I now truly believe that God held me back so I could write this book. There are times when God will say, "Be quiet, be still, and wait on me." God's timing is not always the same as our timing, that's for sure.

After I began to write God's book, I saw his plan unfolding. After a relatively short period of time, God would send me to a published Christian writer. This was meant to help me because I had never written a book before. God sent me to that beautiful lady writer before chapter three was even finished. By chapter five I had a literary agent, and I never thought in a million years that would happen.

God is always at work, and He's always on the clock. He is a spirit that never sleeps. Read Psalms 121 and discover this truth for yourself. God's timetable is not our timetable. Let's do something together, shall we? Let's turn the tables on Satan, and let's take the time to pray. Let's pray and do it often. Let's talk to our Lord. He's listening!

Listen to what Ecclesiastes 8:7 has to say. "Since no man knows the future, who can tell him what is to come?" This scripture would become so true for my family on one summer day in 2000. We were traveling to Indianapolis on Interstate 74 in the eastbound lane when I caught sight of one of the most terrible accidents that I have ever witnessed. The crash had happened just before we arrived, and I pulled to the side of the road and parked our Blazer. I told Cindy and the girls to stay put. I said, "I have to go help." I have seen dead bodies before, but I didn't want them to have to experience it.

It was a terrible accident, with eight to ten vehicles involved. There was debris scattered all over the road, and people were running around in a panic. I think the one thing that bothered me the most was that people were driving through the median and around the accident without stopping. They simply didn't want to help, and they didn't want to wait in traffic. Dozens and dozens of cars did that, and even one eighteen-wheeler.

God was most definitely there that day. Something told me to walk towards a little red sports car. I stuck my head through the passenger side window and saw a young man who appeared to be in his 20s. He was the lone passenger, and he was unconscious.

A young woman who identified herself as a nurse was standing behind the driver and had her arms through the window holding his neck and head up. She said, "This young man will die if I let go of his head. He has severe internal injuries."

I remember looking at the car and the driver and noting that they were both in terrible shape. The driver was bleeding from his mouth, ears, nose, and eye sockets, and the car was not much better. It looked like it had gone through a compactor.

The nurse said, "I smell gas," and I noticed that the car was still running. I yanked the entire key cylinder out of the steering column of that car. God had to be helping me because I'm not that strong. As soon as I removed it, the car stopped running.

I still had my head through the window of the passenger side when I saw a lady standing behind the nurse. She was a white lady and appeared to be about 40 with beautiful brown hair. One thing that I remembered about that day is interesting to me now. That lady never touched the nurse in any way. She did, however, make a statement that I will never forget as long as I live. She said, "Let's pray for this young man." The nurse and I both bowed our heads and this is what she said: "Father, I place this young man's life in your hands. It's not his time to go. Amen."

The nurse and I both said "Amen," and I immediately looked up, but the other woman was nowhere to be found. I looked in both directions but saw no one. I looked at the nurse in amazement and said, "No one can move that fast. I think we just witnessed an angel."

The nurse looked at me and said, "I believe you're right."

By that time the driver was starting to go into convulsions, and the nurse cried out, "You have to get this door open. It's broken!" I ran around to her side and jerked the door off of its hinges. Once again, it had to be God. As soon as I got the door off and out of the way, two paramedics arrived. One of them looked at us and said, "You probably saved his life." I remember hugging the nurse and walking away. I never thought to ask the nurse her name, and I never saw her again.

I walked back to my car and family, and I drove away

crying. The first thing that I did was to tell my wife and kids that I loved them. Then I told them what happened. We tried to find out that young man's name and which hospital he was taken to, but were unable to do so. Young man, if you are reading this book, please call me! God spared you for a reason and I want to be a part of your life.

I'll end with these thoughts. Jesus is calling all of us to repentance, but Satan has manufactured a lie that he likes to spread around. He wants you to think that you can ask Jesus to forgive you of your sins anytime, and that you don't have to do it now. He says that you have all the time in the world, but you don't. Remember, God's timetable is not always the same as ours.

Chapter Seven

Insurance—Who Needs It?

It is wise to have an insurance policy on your property before you even begin building a home on it. Lending institutions require a homeowner's policy on a home before they will lend money to build it. This policy insures the land, the house, and any out buildings that may be present, and also protects the owner from being held liable if an accident occurs. Whether you realize it or not, God has a life insurance policy on you. You are the beneficiary, but can you guess who the policyholder is? If you guessed Jesus, you were right. Jesus paid for your policy with nothing less than His blood.

When you have to borrow the money to build a new home, like most of us do, you will have what is called a mortgage. A mortgage is a financial contract between the lending institution and the individual who borrows from them. Mortgages outline payment terms, the monthly amount due, and the number of months or years that it will take to repay the loan. Almost all mortgages are written so the payment is due on the first of the month. I'm not sure why lending institutions do it that way, but I'm sure they have a reason for it. I do know that if you don't make your payments on time it can definitely damage your credit. Every time you are late with a payment your mortgage holder will report it to the credit bureau, and it will go on your credit report. If you get behind on payments, your mortgage holder will repossess your house. In other words, you can lose your home.

There is a lot of paperwork involved in borrowing money. Most of this is dictated by the Federal Truth-in-Lending Laws. When you apply for a mortgage, the lending institution will perform what is called a title search. A property title is much like a title for a vehicle and is called a deed. When you have a mortgage you will also have a title insurance policy. Title insurance companies research the history of the property, looking for liens and judgments that may have been placed on it. The title insurance company insures that the property is free and clear, and if it turns out not to be so, they can be held liable.

I have done many jobs that were financed by banks, many of whom wanted me to sign lien waivers. A lien waiver is a legal document that states the bank will pay all money due the contractor if he waves his legal lien rights. Contractors should never sign these documents. I signed a lien waiver once and got badly burned as a result. You should learn from the mistakes of others, since you can't live long enough to make them all yourself.

When I begin to write each chapter, I research the Bible for scriptures that apply to the subject matter. As I was searching for material for this chapter, I came across John 17:11-15. Jesus was praying to the Father for His disciples in these verses, but He could have just as easily been talking about you and I, or our lost loved ones. I truly hope these scriptures will help you if you lost a loved one on September 11, 2001.

John 17:11-15 reads as follows:

I will remain in the world no longer, but they are still in the world, and I am coming to you. Holy Father, protect them by the power of your name-the name you gave me-so that they may be one as we are one. While

I was with them, I protected them and kept them safe by that name you gave me. None has been lost except the one doomed to destruction so that scripture would be fulfilled. I am coming to you now, but I say these things while I am still in the world, so that they may have the full measure of my joy within them. I have given them your word and the world has hated them, for they are not of the world any more than I am of the world. My prayer is not that you take them out of the world but that you protect them from the evil one.

God's Protection

I'd like to tell you a humorous story about our oldest daughter. Randie was about four or five years old, and we had just moved into our first home. We were living in the country and we had been snowed in for a couple of days. Randie was getting cabin fever, so she asked if she could go outside and play. I told her that I didn't think it was such a good idea, but my wife thought something totally different.

Cindy said, "Oh, let her go."

I said, "It's snowing out there, and it's drifting badly."

"Oh, let her go! She's just a kid who wants to have some fun," was my wife's response.

Reluctantly, I said, "Okay."

Cindy put so many clothes on Randie that she could have stocked the shelves of the Goodwill store with them. I remember standing at the front door watching Randie walk about ten feet. I could see that she had a false sense of security as she walked on top of a rather large snowdrift that was covered with a thin layer of ice. I remember her looking at me and smiling and waving. She was having a great time, or so she thought.

Suddenly the snowdrift gave way and Randie fell in up to her neck. The only thing I could see was her head. You might think that a parent would panic and run outside, but I didn't. I knew it wasn't life threatening, and the sight of her head sticking out of that snowdrift struck me as being funny.

Randie started to cry and said, "Please, don't let me die out here!" Cindy saw what was going on and said, "Go out there and help her!" I put my coat on and went outside, pulled Randie out of the snow drift, brushed her off, and took her back inside. Once I gave her some hot chocolate, she was fine.

I don't want you to think I'm picking on Randie, but I have another story about her that illustrates how God protects his children in more ways than we can imagine. When you finished chapter three you may have been left with some questions about Randie that weren't answered. Back in chapter three, I shared how Randie hit a deer and totaled her car, but thankfully she was unhurt.

Randie's insurance policy had run out, but I wasn't aware of it. Randie may not have been in the good hands of Allstate, but she was in the good hands of the Father, who watches over us and protects us. As any parent, I was more concerned about Randie's well being than the car. I went with her to get an estimate on the damages. We went to a gentleman who had done bodywork for us before, and whom I have always viewed as an honest and decent man.

The man gave us the estimate, which totaled over $5000. Then he asked, "Which insurance company do I bill?"

I said, "Bill me."

Of course, he asked, "Why?"

I had to tell him of my embarrassing mistake, but I never told him that I didn't have the money. I didn't know how, but I knew that God would provide a way to fix Randie's car. I figured that the man would laugh at me, but he didn't. Our new-found friend stared at me, and I could tell that wheels were spinning in his head, and he was thinking hard about something.

Our friend offered to repair Randie's car free if I installed a new roof on his house, and I said, "It will cost more than $5000 to put a new roof on your house."

His response was, "That's okay, I'll pay you the difference."

To make a long story short, we installed a new roof on the man's house, and I still made a profit on the job. And the most amazing part of this story is I didn't offer the deal, but our friend did. I took an insurance damage claim to the Lord in prayer and He paid it, plus I got a refund check. Try to get that kind of coverage from Allstate.

I'd like to tell you another story. My company was building a new home on the east side of Indianapolis in the summer of 2000 and on this day we were working on the foundation. We were pulling a cement mixer behind our pickup on Interstate 70 during morning rush hour. I was talking to Randie while I was driving, and suddenly I noticed that our mixer was passing us. I had to speed up because it was going to sideswipe us. I watched our mixer in the rear view mirror, and by that time, all four lanes of traffic saw what was going on. With sparks flying out of the mounting plate, the mixer traveled about a quarter of a mile in a straight line until it gently tapped the guardrail and fell over on its side. We pulled over to the side of the road and tried to set the mixer back up on its wheels, but Randie and I were simply not strong enough to lift it. Two strangers saw our difficulty and stopped to lend a hand. Eventually, all four of us got the mixer back on its wheels and I thanked our helpers.

As it turned out, the mixer suffered no damage, and we were only five minutes late for work. A pin had broken off in the towing tube of the mixer. While the tube remained attached to the ball on the truck bumper, the mixer had detached and gotten away from us. It wasn't a laughing matter at the time, but it is now. Nothing bad happened, but it easily could have if the Lord hadn't had His hand of protection on us. There could have been a tragic accident, but thank God it didn't happen.

Sometimes the best insurance policy in the world is not enough. That was the case during the construction of our company's first new home in 1993. We were to construct a two-story home that was in the quarter of a million dollar range. Things were going well on this house, or so I thought. I would end up breaking both my feet on that job and losing all of my on-site tools and a backhoe. All on one job! It wasn't a good start to the dream of a new home construction business, was it?

We have cargo construction trailers that we haul to the job site in which we store our tools. During the construction of this particular home, someone cut the locks off the trailer and stole all of the tools. Naturally, I turned in an insurance claim, but my agent said our tools weren't covered on our policy. He said I needed what was called a tool waiver. I had never had one, nor had he ever told me that I had needed one. The homeowner's agent refused to pay for the loss also. We filled out a police report, but no one was ever arrested for the crime. I eventually replaced the tools, but it was a difficult out-of-pocket expense for the company. You might say the moral of this story is not to look to your insurance company for your security. Only the Lord can provide true security.

Winds of Change

The Lord has been saying that the winds of change are coming, and I would like to share a story with you about wind. A few years ago, an accountant hired us to construct a large pole barn on his property. He was a horse lover and planned to use the barn as a riding arena, but the discouraging part of this story is it took the customer three tries before he saw his dream fulfilled.

The owner first contacted my company in the fall of 1995. He had hired a contractor to construct his arena, but was dissatisfied with what had happened. Everything had gone well with the framework, but when it came time to install the sheet metal on the walls and roof, extremely high winds toppled the building's frame. Although the structure was still standing, it was leaning at a 45° angle. I told him that if we constructed the building, the existing structure would first have to be taken apart. He agreed with that stipulation, and we signed a contract.

We began to disassemble the structure and rebuild it.

Once again, everything went well with the framework until it came time for installation of the sheet metal. We arrived at the job site one day and found disaster had happened once again. A minor tornado had swept over that structure, and the treated 6' x 6' posts that were cemented four feet into the ground were broken off like toothpicks. The stacks of sheet metal were scattered across the adjacent fields like paper, and everything that we had done was ruined. The owner paid us, but acquired the services of another contractor to construct his building for the third time. I guess you might say that the third time is a charm because the building was finished and it's standing today. It's a beautiful building, but it goes to show you that nature is unpredictable.

The Lord promises to help us and protect us. He kept His promise when I was in the hospital with blood clots when He spared my life and I'm grateful for that. I'm also glad we had medical insurance during that hospital stay. My in-patient stay lasted twelve days at a cost of $39,000, but our out-of-pocket expenses were only $1000. The Lord guaranteed the writing of this book by sparing His servant's life, and I thank Him and praise His holy name for it.

First Corinthians 13:6,7 says, "Love does not delight in evil but rejoices with the truth. It always protects, always trusts, always hopes, always perseveres." Although it appeared to my mother that she wouldn't see her boys again, God was going to make sure that she would. When God closes one door He always opens another one. My mother and I now call each other on a daily basis and we are the best of friends. However, friendship does not seem to be in the cards for my father and me.

Our God is a God of love, and if you don't walk in that love like God's children should, you will choose your own destiny. Satan's heart is filled with evil, and he ignores love. He also knows that his days are numbered, and that he has cemented his damnation forever by rejecting God's love. Don't make the same mistake that Satan did. Walk in God's love and you won't regret it.

Jesus said in Matthew 24:7: "Nation will rise against nation, and kingdom against kingdom. There will be famines and earthquakes in various places." Jesus was warning us of things that would come about before His return. If you take notice of our global weather changes, you'll see that it's no coincidence. The Lord is demonstrating that His word is true. Even Satan knows that the Lord's Word is true, and that He will return soon. That's why he seeks to devour those whom he can, so please, don't be a midnight snack for the enemy.

A short time ago, I was driving to Lafayette to see our pastor. Before I reached the city limits, I noticed something unusual. In the front yard of a home was a rather large elm tree that had been broken off at the ground like it was nothing. In the backyard of the same home was a barn that had been reduced to toothpicks. I found it unusual that there were no visible signs of damage anywhere else, not even to the house, and I remember telling my pastor what I had seen and what the Lord had impressed on me. I told him, "If the owner knew that disaster was coming, they would have been prepared for the worst." Jesus is indeed coming back for His chosen people, and once again I say, be prepared.

God's plan of salvation is the master insurance policy, and it's your claim to heaven. God's Word says that no one can come to the Father except through Jesus. If you don't want to take my word for it, then read it in the Bible for yourself. Time is short, so let Jesus claim your heart and your life. Don't be left behind when He returns.

God has a way of turning things into learning lessons and making them interesting, that's for sure. I'll leave you with the following thought: God has an insurance policy on your life, and it's called the blood of Jesus. You had a claim for restoration, and Jesus paid it in full.

Chapter Eight

How Do I Pay For It?

Since this chapter deals with money issues, I think it would be wise and appropriate for me to thank you for your purchase of this book. Believe me, your book purchase will help God's children in more ways than you can imagine, and it is my sincere hope that you are working on becoming a builder of the spirit yourself. I hope you're enjoying the book, as it's truly a labor of love. Now, let's roll up our sleeves, put on our thinking caps, and figure out how to pay for a building project.

Constructing a new home can be rather expensive. Very rarely do we ever construct a home for less than $100,000, so like most people, our customers have to borrow the money. If you are in the position to pay cash for your home, you're better off than most, but I know very few people who can do it.

Most mortgages for new home construction run 30 years in length, and that's a lot of interest. Most people don't realize it, but you will end up paying back far more in interest than you will principal. Since most people focus all their attention on the monthly payment, they fail to examine the entire financing picture.

Let's look at an example of new home financing. If you purchase a home for $100,000, at an interest rate of 7%, you will pay back a total of $310,000 over 30 years. That means you would have 360 payments, with each one being $861.11. You will be paying $7,000 a year in interest alone, and over 30 years, you will have paid $210,000 in interest. Believe me, most lending institutions only want you to focus on the monthly payment, and don't want you to look at the whole picture.

I have never claimed to be a financial expert, but I do know this much: when you borrow money, you become a slave to the lender. That statement comes from the Bible. If you don't believe it, just get behind on your payments and then you'll see what I'm talking about. God wants us to be good stewards with the money that He has given us, and when it comes to the decision of going into debt, always pray about it first. I truly feel in my spirit that hard times are coming, so if you're in debt, you'd better get out and stay out.

There are certain individuals in society who can't afford things, so they steal them. There are numerous scriptures that caution about this type of behavior. In fact, "Thou shalt not steal," is one of the Ten Commandments, and you'll find it in Exodus 20:15.

I truly believe that evil spirits can oppress people and force them to do things out of their normal character. I hope this next story will help you to recognize this. Remember, Satan never comes to the front door and knocks. He crawls through the back window that you left barely cracked open. What I'm trying to say is that we need to watch the behavior of people. Sometimes individuals do things and they don't know why, but the Holy Spirit always knows why. Don't accept a strange spirit into your house or the house of another. The house that I am speaking of is your temple, and the Bible says that you are a temple of the Holy Ghost. We are to pray strange spirits out and close the window of opportunity that they used for entry.

I would like to point out that I do not recall any part of

this story, but my mother told me about it, and I believe her because she is a woman of truth. She said that I was in the third grade when my teacher sent word to her that I was stealing everything I could get my hands on. My teacher seriously felt I was headed for reform school, so naturally my mother was concerned and set up an appointment to go in and talk with her. Mom said that when she asked me if I was stealing, I didn't deny it. She said my exact words were, "Mommy, I don't know why I steal things."

Mom decided that she'd better pray. The Lord told her to fast for three days, and she did as He advised. She promised the Lord that if He removed that stealing spirit from me, she would witness to my teacher and tell her about Jesus. After the third day of fasting, Mom paid a visit to my teacher. The teacher couldn't understand why I stole things, because she thought I was a nice boy. Mom told the teacher that she had prayed about it and that God was going to remedy the problem. The teacher said she believed her, and that was Mom's open door invitation to witness. If we watch and listen, the Lord will open the door to witness, but we need to recognize when the door opens and walk through it before it closes.

Mom jumped on that opportunity and witnessed to my teacher. She told her about Jesus and kept the promise she had made to God. Mom said my teacher began to cry. She said that she believed in the things of the Lord and agreed with my mom for God to lift that spirit of stealing from me. And He did!

Stealing From God

Let's talk about stealing of a spiritual nature. Contrary to what you may believe, withholding your tithes is stealing from God. God's Word says you shall not place any other gods before Him, but if money is more important to you than anything else, you have a new god. The Bible is filled with stories about money. Some of the stories are good and some are bad. Look what happened to Judas. He hung himself over 30 pieces of silver. Money can literally cause an untimely death.

If you desire to live for the Lord, you must pay tithes. How can you expect God to bless you when you cheat him? Let's look at what God has to say about working and paying your fair share. 1 Timothy 6:10 says, "For the love of money is the root of all kinds of evil. Some people, eager for money, have wandered from the faith and pierced themselves with many griefs." Did you notice that Paul emphasized the point that the *love* of money is the root problem, and not money itself?

I pay 10% of my gross wages to the Lord. Remember when I said that you cheat the Lord by not paying your tithes? I read an article once that said only 10% of all church members pay tithes as they should. The individuals who don't pay their fair share can't figure out why their finances are a disaster. Perhaps it's because 90% of the church is walking in disobedience. Start paying your tithes and you will see a change in your finances.

Paying for Our Actions

Let's shift gears and talk about the consequences one must pay for their actions. God's Word says to obey the laws of the land, and we are told in Numbers 32:23 that you can be sure that your sin will find you out. Those who break the law will certainly be judged, and Leviticus 26:43 tells us that they will pay for their sins because they have rejected God's laws and detested His decrees.

Terre Haute, Indiana, is a small midwestern town with a population of about 50,000. My family and I live approximately 50 miles from there, along the Wabash River on the western border of the state. It's a normal town in most respects, but one significant difference is that it contains a federal penitentiary.

In the summer of 2001, Terre Haute was the showcase of the world. Timothy McVeigh, the Oklahoma City bomber, was executed there in July for his crimes against humanity. We know that he murdered hundreds of innocent men, women, and children, but it is hard to understand why he would have done such a thing. People are still asking why he would have committed such a terrible act. I think it's because he had a terrible hatred for the United States government, and he acted on his emotions. I truly believe that Timothy McVeigh was motivated by a higher power than himself, and I'm not talking about our Lord.

Many people asked if he was sorry for what he did. Only the Lord can really answer that, but everything that I have read and seen suggests that he wasn't. If he had experienced true repentance in his heart, we would have known it. Those of us who remain have only two choices. We can either forgive him, or we can harbor the same type of resentment that he had, which will, in turn, pull us down. I know it's hard to forgive someone for such actions, but we must. Mr. McVeigh paid for his crimes on this earth with his life and if he didn't ask Jesus to forgive him of his sins, he will pay for them again in hell. If you were affected by this terrible crime, you must move on. I know what you may think, "That's easy for you to say," but our Lord said this year is one of restoration. It's restoration time for you, my friend. Timothy McVeigh is gone, and his life and actions are only a memory now. Remember that God can restore what Satan has stolen, so keep the good memories of your loved one or friend in your heart and mind.

Romans 6:23 tells us that, "The wages of sin is death, but the gift of God is eternal life in Christ Jesus our Lord." I know it may be hard to understand, but even the most hardened criminals can be forgiven. If they ask Jesus to come into their heart and forgive them of their sins he will give them a spiritual pardon. They may still lose their lives as a consequence of their actions, but they will be released from confinement when they get to heaven. We are the ones who have a hard time with forgiveness, but it's never been a problem for our Lord.

Only one week after Timothy McVeigh was executed, another prisoner faced the same fate. The second execution was that of a convicted drug dealer who murdered two individuals. I can't say where that poor soul is resting, but I can say that the Lord would have forgiven him of his sins if he had only asked. Only the prisoner and his Creator know if that confession occurred. I remember seeing that prisoner's little girl beg for her father's life on national television. She cried while asking the President to pardon her dad, but the pardon never came and the man's soul was thrust into eternity. I truly hope that his spirit is now residing in the light and not in the darkness.

Let's shift gears once again and study the behavior of individuals who aren't really considered evil, but who have corrupted morals. They may get away with their deeds in this life, but they won't in the next one. The Lord once showed me what individuals like this have in store for them if they don't repent.

My family and I were traveling on Interstate 75 through Kentucky on our way back from vacation when the Lord decided to communicate with me in a rather unique and humbling way. We were driving along when I noticed that the gas gauge was on empty, so we had no choice but to take the next exit and refuel. That particular exit just happened to be the one where my father lived, and we pulled into the gas station and began to fill up. I remember looking up the road that went to my father's residence and feeling the Spirit of God consume my entire being. I told my wife to continue filling the car and that I would be detained for a few minutes.

I walked behind the filling station and experienced something beyond words that I never care to experience again. The Lord showed me a vision of what would be in store for those who reject Him. It's truly hard to describe that vision and what I experienced. I felt total emptiness in my soul, and the loneliness and darkness that consumed me was absolutely unbearable. The Lord placed that feeling in my Spirit for only a matter of seconds, but it felt like an eternity. I couldn't stand it, and I begged Him to remove it from me.

If you haven't asked Jesus to come into your heart and forgive you of your sins, now is the time. Believe me, you don't want to experience what I did in my vision. If we're away from the Father we are totally alone, and mere words can never explain that horrible, emptiness.

Now let's ask ourselves the question, "How did Jesus pay for it?" The answer is that He paid for the sins of the world by sacrificing Himself so that we could live.

In 1987 I was working at a local factory when a severe winter storm hit. Blizzard conditions began to develop and the authorities ordered the roads closed. Management at the factory told us to head out, so I phoned home and heard panic on the other end of the line. Cindy said she and the girls were freezing to death. She told me that they were out of fuel oil and that she had tacked a blanket over the kitchen door, and was trying to keep herself and the kids warm with the heat generating from the burners on the kitchen stove.

When I left for home, I didn't know at the time that it would be a dangerous adventure. I was driving a pickup truck and that gave me a small sense of security. My house was roughly 15 miles from work, but the drive felt more like 100 miles.

People were abandoning their vehicles right in the middle of the road, and several vehicles had been pushed into the ditch by snowplows. I remember speeding up to 60 mph and hitting drifts, which would reduce my speed to about 20 mph before I could speed up again. I knew that if I could get through the "S" curve in New Ross, which drifts the worst, I would be able to make it.

Don't ask me how, but I made it to the curve. The drifts in the right lane were eight to ten feet tall, so I floored it and hoped for the best. There's a set of railroad tracks right in the center of that curve, and as I was speeding down the wrong side of the road I saw something that I will never forget—a car parked on the railroad tracks. I tapped on my brakes but there was no response. I was driving on a solid sheet of ice, and I knew that I was not going to be able to stop. I tried to get past the car using the right lane, but the drifting snow kept pushing me into the left lane. As I got closer, I saw I was actually going to clear the vehicle. Just as I began to pass the car, I saw a man standing next to it. He jumped backwards and pinned himself to the side of the car and I saw my truck mirror miss his face by inches. The momentum of my passing him threw my truck into the drift, and I immediately ran to see if I had injured him. When I got there, there was a woman alongside him standing in the middle of the road, and they were wearing only windbreakers. It was quite obvious that they were both high on drugs.

Now I was really starting to panic. I knew that, although those two didn't die from a traffic accident, they would eventually die from exposure to the elements. I told the gentleman and his friend to get in my truck and asked him if he was all right.

He said, "Yes, why wouldn't I be?"

I said, "Don't you realize that I almost killed you?"

His exact words were, "It wasn't that close, was it?"

I asked him why he stopped on the tracks, and he said he had felt that he couldn't make it any farther. When I asked him why he hadn't turned his emergency flashers on, he said he didn't want to run his battery down.

So there I was, stranded in the middle of nowhere, with two freezing druggies in a blizzard. As we were walking to my truck, two state highway snowplows arrived. I remember both trucks stopping and the drivers rolling down their windows. They yelled, "Get out of the way, we have orders to plow everything into the ditch!"

I stood in front of the lead truck and told the driver, "I have a life and death situation at home, and I have to get there!" I told him that I was desperate and not going to move. I remember saying, "You will have to kill me!"

The driver of the second plow told the lead driver to pull me out, but the lead driver said he would have to radio into headquarters to ask permission to do it. He called them but they refused.

I looked at the lead driver and said, "I'm not moving!"

Neither of the drivers liked it, but they pulled my truck from the drift. I asked the lead driver what he planned to do with the intoxicated couple, and he said he would take them home. I thanked the drivers, got in my truck, and drove home. When I walked into the house, I found Cindy and the girls in the kitchen, where they were huddled over the stove. It was so cold in the house that there were icicles hanging from the showerhead in the bathroom.

First I had to find the problem with the furnace. I walked over to the furnace, looked at it and flipped the power switch on. One of the kids had accidentally turned the power switch off on the furnace. The furnace ran fine and the house warmed up quickly. I told Cindy, "I almost killed a man tonight for this!"

Now that I have time to think about it, I would say that man is lucky to be alive. He almost paid for his drug habit with his life, and I truly thank God that I didn't kill him. I would have had to live with that memory the rest of my life, and he would have been cheated out of the fullness of his own life.

I'll leave you with this thought. People who have wronged you in the past may get away with it in this lifetime, but they will have to face it when they stand before the Lord on judgment day. The ones who have lied, cheated, and stolen will have to give account for that, and if they haven't asked Jesus to forgive them of their sins before that day comes, they will pay for it forever.

CHAPTER NINE

How Do We Measure Up?

Since the dawn of time, man has desired to measure his existence, and God created us with a spirit that longs for that knowledge. The universe is filled with God's glory, much of which science cannot explain. His divine plan is that we constantly search for the truth, but He will never give us all the pieces to the puzzle because if He did, we would never need to wonder or search again. We are limited in our understanding of our Creator, and that may be the reason why He birthed curiosity in us.

Our Christian walk is constantly measured, both by the Holy Spirit and those around us. There are questions that you probably ask yourself. "How does my life measure up? Is it my desire to be measured by man or by the Spirit? Is my life set to a high standard or is it lacking? Do I lead or do I follow?" The bottom line is, are you using God's Word to measure your life or are you looking to the world for answers?

There are literally thousands of measuring devices that exist today. We measure things like time, temperature, and rainfall and we can even measure the rise and fall of the oceans. The three main measuring devices used when constructing a new home are tape measures, squares, and levels.

The smallest unit of measure on a tape measure is 1/32 of an inch, but there are devices that can measure hundreds or even thousands of an inch. There's even one on the market today that is helpful for those of us who are forgetful, and it's called the "Talking Tape Measure." It's constructed with a tape recorder inside to record your voice. When you need to remember the measurements you took, you just play back your voice. Pretty clever!

Squares are simply devices that help us mark out a 90° angle to a reference surface. There are many different types of squares, but the two main types that we use are framing squares and drywall squares.

There are also several different types of levels, ranging from a few inches to several feet in length. A popular level is one called a "transit" level. This type of level measures the grade of the ground, that is, the levelness of the soil. Transit levels can either be of the conventional or the laser type.

The night before I began to write this chapter, God chose to use something rather small as a measuring device. While I was using the restroom I noticed a bobby pin on the floor. When I picked it up, something told me to bend it flat. After I flattened it, I began to understand what the Lord was saying. When a bobby pin is bent flat it has two sides. One side is flat and the other side is wavy and crooked. The Lord spoke very clearly and told me that the bobby pin was a learning tool.

I immediately ran to the living room and asked my girls what they saw in that pin. Two of them said, "It's a bobby pin." One said, "It's a flattened bobby pin which has two sides. One side is straight and the other is crooked." I told them that their Christian walk was just like that bobby pin, and I asked them, "Which side best describes your Christian walk?" Two said the wavy side and one said the straight side. I told them that truly serving the Lord is never a straight path, but rather it's full of waves.

God chose, of all things, a bobby pin to teach us. He said in 1 Corinthians 1:27 that He would use the foolish things of this world to shame the wise. Most of us may think that using a bobby pin as a learning tool would be foolish, but that's probably why God chose to use it.

Find a bobby pin, flatten it, and then tape it somewhere. Put it on your refrigerator, in your car, on your desk or beside your bed. Place it where you will be able to see it each day, and it will be a constant reminder to you of how you should measure up.

Some of you are probably asking, "How do we measure our lives?" We measure our lives by using God's Word, which is our standard. Put that spirit of curiosity to good use and let your fingers do the walking. Micah 6:8 is a good scripture to use when measuring strengths and weaknesses.

Is your walk with the Lord full of ease, or is it full of waves? If you think your walk with the Lord is going to be like a calm ocean, think again. You must always remember that Satan is your enemy and he loves to make waves in your life.

I have always been fascinated with the lives of the Amish who are a Protestant sect of people noted for their simplicity of living and their refusal to take oaths or bear arms. I view them as hard workers who are trying to set a standard of morality, and I admire them for it.

The Amish are famous for their barn raisings. When a neighbor has a need, everyone in the community pulls together to accomplish the task. The men work together to raise the structure, and the women cook the meals for the men. God's Word says that we are to help those in need, and I think we could learn a lot from them. When you help one of God's children, it's pleasing to Him.

I recently attended a morning service at our church where the pastor asked if a plumber in the audience could lend a hand on one of the church projects. He said to contact one of the assistant pastors after the service, so I talked to him and he described what was needed. The church had purchased a small home and it needed its entire bathroom remodeled, but I got the impression that they wanted it done for free. That's fine if someone desires to volunteer their services, but this was a massive project that would take two or three weeks to complete. I told the assistant pastor that I would do the project for free if the Lord told me to, but that He hadn't. The assistant pastor said, "We'll get back with you," and I left it at that.

My wife gave me a hard time because I didn't do the work voluntarily, but I repeatedly told her, "God hasn't told me to do it for free." During my attendance at other churches people often took advantage of me because they knew I owned a construction company. I had been very naive in the past and had believed everybody when they said they were down on their luck. The truth, however, was they were too stingy to pay for it, and they had taken advantage of me. I told the Lord that I would never be placed in a position like that again, so I now pray for guidance before each job. I don't understand the thought process of some churches and organizations that think they should get everything for free. Why don't those organizations pray for the wisdom to enable them to pay for it? It's a different matter when someone wants to volunteer their time and money for a cause, but it's wrong to feel pressured into doing something out of a sense of guilt.

The maintenance man of the church called me and said that they wanted an estimate to remodel the bathroom, which really surprised me. I gave them the estimate and they accepted it about a week later. I gave them a reduced rate for the work, but God never told me to do it for free. We remodeled the bathroom in roughly two and a half weeks and received a lot of comments on our high quality of work even from the pastor.

Organizations Can Stifle God's Purposes

I would like to make something perfectly clear. I'm not a Republican or a Democrat. I'm an Independent who votes for the person and not the party. The church we attend has a denominational label, but my family and I attend that church because God told me to go there. Denominational labels mean nothing to me. Manmade rules can handicap what God wants to do.

My family and I had a yard sale recently, and we tried to donate the remaining items to the local thrift store that is owned by one of the denominational ministries. We became so frustrated with that store that we gave the items to a worldly thrift store organization instead. That store was far more organized than our church thrift store was.

The point I'm trying to make is that we can be torn down by organization. Believe it or not, being too organized can be a bad thing. If you're in a position of authority, like I am, you should let most of your employees make their own decisions. If they don't feel comfortable with making a decision, they'll come to you for advice. If God tells you to do something, do it. We learned in Chapter Six that God's timing is everything, so if you wait and ask permission, it may be too late.

I am not encouraging anyone to rebel against their pastor or authority. That's not God's will, but my point is that you will never go wrong by obeying God. He may instruct you to do something totally opposite of what your boss has said to do, but your response should be dictated by who you fear the most. Do you fear the Lord, or do you fear losing your job?

If something isn't working and we're in a rut, we need to pray for a solution to the problem. The Word says that if a man lacks wisdom, he should ask, so I always pray for wisdom. Jesus tells us in Matthew 26: 41 to "Watch and pray so that we don't fall into temptation. The spirit is willing but the body is weak." Some of us can't seem to get out of the rut and continually fall in holes over and over again. We say, "That's the way we've always done it," but in reality it's probably not God's way at all. If the Lord were to give us advice, He would probably say, "Climb out of that rut, I have a new way!" Dust yourself off and fill that rut in. It's time to move on with a higher plan.

During the winter of 2000, my family and I attended our first Christian skate night. The event was held at one of the local roller-skating rinks in Indianapolis, and a local Christian radio station was sponsoring it. The radio station was selling CDs called, "Album Project 2000." The CD consisted of songs by local Christian talent, so we purchased one and I listened to it the next day.

Although all of the songs were good, I was especially drawn to one of them. Every time I heard that song I cried uncontrollably, so I felt moved by the Spirit to write the young lady who wrote it. I didn't know her address, but I found the address and phone number of the recording studio where the CD was recorded. The recording studio was located only a few miles away, so I sent a letter to the owner. I didn't go into great detail but I did tell him that the Lord gave me a tremendous word of encouragement for that lady.

To be honest with you, I never thought I would hear from him, but I was narrow-minded and didn't quite measure up to the task. When God tells you to do something you better believe, and do it. God's always working, but we just don't always see it. Shortly after I mailed the letter, I received a message on my answering machine. It was the recording studio owner, who said that he knew God's hand was in this because the young lady needed encouragement. The studio owner gave me her address, and I mailed her a letter. I basically told her that she had touched my life with her song and thanked her. I also told her that God was going to move in her life in a mighty way. Although I haven't heard from her, I know that it was God working. I obeyed the Lord's instructions and the studio owner did as well.

I think we can all learn from 2 John :6. That scripture tells us, "And this is love: That we walk in obedience to his commands. As you heard from the beginning, his demand is that you walk in love."

My sincere prayer for that young lady is that the Lord will move in her life in a mighty way. I wouldn't serve this story justice if I didn't include the words to her song. It's called "All I Wanna Do!"

(Chorus)
All I wanna do is love You
All I wanna do is lay down at Your feet and weep

All I wanna see is Your face smilin' down on me
All I wanna do Lord is love You
I can't find a way to tell of my love for You
I just wanna hold You in my arms.
There will come a day when we'll see each other face to face
Maybe I'll have the words to say, I don't know but that's okay
But for now Lord.
(Chorus)
This world you know leaves you feelin' so empty and hollow
It tears your soul apart and it leaves you standing bare
I'm tired of the stale sermons
I'm tired of the weak worship
I'm tired of the powerless church
I'm tired of being void of You
All we need Lord is more of You
If You don't touch us Lord surely we will die inside
All we really need is a mighty, mighty, mighty awakening
All we really need Lord, is more of You!

I believe that Julie is truly a builder. She has built my spirit up in more ways than she can imagine, and I hope you can now understand why her song makes me cry every time I hear it.

Remember when I told you that Katie and I were going to restore a 1966 Ford Mustang? Well, that car may not look like much, but we see potential in it where others can't. God always sees potential in each of us, no matter what the circumstances are, and He touches the heart of his children in different ways.

I must give Katie credit. She always sees potential in her friends. Proverbs 13:20 states, "He who walks with the wise grows wise, but the comparison of fools suffers harm." I'm hoping that the first part of that scripture comes true for one of Katie's friends. As you may recall Katie is our youngest daughter. She has many friends but there's one particular girl in whom Katie has always seen potential. Recently, the girl invited Katie out to dinner for a talk, and that was Katie's opportunity to witness for Christ. She told her friend that she never looks happy.

Her friend asked, "What's your secret to happiness?"

Katie answered, "Jesus lives in my heart, and when I got saved He turned my life around and He can do the same for you!"

Her friend said in a humble voice, "I'll think about it."

I told Katie that she had done the right thing by planting the thought of salvation in her friend's mind. The Holy Spirit will water that thought. First Corinthians 16:13 and 14 says, "Be on your guard; stand firm in the faith; be men of courage; be strong. Do everything in love!" I think we can all learn from Katie and her friend. It just goes to show you that people are constantly watching you and your life.

Dave Wilkerson, a well-respected minister in New York City, sends out monthly newsletters. One of them was entitled, "The Towers Have Fallen But We Missed The Message." In his letter he states, "Even now the Lord is raising up godly watchmen to speak for him in these times." My given name is Gregory, which means "watchman," and now I'm speaking for the Lord in print.

Now I'd like to talk about individuals who only call on the Lord in times of trouble. When the trouble passes and they are out of the woods, they go right back to living in sin. Someone I know, who lives in another state, discovered that he had cancer. He had never really desired to live for the Lord until then. When the doctor told him he had cancer, he immediately began to call people for prayer. God answered those prayers and the cancer disappeared. Afterward, he went back to living his old lifestyle, and guess what? The cancer's back, and once again he's really praying. We have talked to him repeatedly about his salvation, and he says he knows the way and is saved, but I'm really skeptical about it. Isaiah 30:21 tells us that, "Whether you turn to the right or to the left, your ears will hear a voice behind you, saying, this is the way; walk in it." It's my sincere prayer that he will hear that voice.

1 John 1:8-10 tells us that,

*If we claim to be without sin, we deceive ourselves
and the truth is not in us. If we confess our sins, he is
faithful and just and will forgive us from all unrighteousness. If we claim we have not sinned, we make
him out to be a liar and his word has no place in our
lives.*

Is your life level and full of righteousness, or is it tilted
with sin? Are you out of square and running away from the
Lord? Romans 3:23 and 24 tell us that we all fall short of the
glory of God but that we can be forgiven.

You might be thinking that you don't measure up and
you're not worthy. Satan would like for you to think that and
run away from God's presence, but remember this: None of us
are worthy of anything, but God sees potential in us and that's
why John 3:16 was written. "For God so loved the world that
he gave his one and only son, that whosoever believes in him
shall not perish but have eternal life." No matter where you
measure on God's spiritual yardstick, He will always love you
and see potential in you.

CHAPTER TEN

The Basement of Life!

In this chapter, we're going to talk about one component of a foundation, although our focus isn't really going to be on foundations at all. The focus of this chapter is about the trials and tribulations of everyday life. I think most of us are familiar with what basements are. In the construction industry, there are three main types of foundational support: basements, crawl spaces, and concrete slabs.

Although concrete slabs are almost always specified in commercial buildings, they are becoming very popular in the home construction industry as well. A concrete slab is typically 4" thick, lies on top of the ground, and forms the floor of your home. Crawl spaces are areas under your home that aren't considered basements because they are uninhabitable. Crawl spaces are typically excavated anywhere from 18" to 36" deep and consist of concrete block walls which have foundation vents installed for air circulation. They almost always have a pea gravel base, which is poured directly on top of the ground. A basement is typically considered a luxury item when constructing a home because it is the most expensive type of support feature to construct. Basements are the areas under your home that give you the ability to walk around, and are sometimes even converted into living space. They are typically eight to ten feet deep, and usually have 8" thick poured concrete walls. There are numerous advantages to a basement if you can afford it.

Now I'd like to discuss backfill. If you're not familiar with that term, it means to fill in the void or space that remains around the exterior foundation walls. After excavation of the soil is complete and the foundation walls are done, the time comes to backfill around the perimeter with dirt. To put it in simple terms, you're leveling the ground out. The open void in the ground looks pretty ugly until its backfilled, but after it is complete, things look much better.

Backfilling can also describe your life before Christ. To begin with, life is full of voids and is ugly. Then you meet Jesus. Our Savior loves to work with dirt, and He's an expert on backfill. When you ask Him to be the Lord of your life, you are no longer ugly or dirty. You became transformed into something of beauty.

Jesus tells us in John 14:1 to do the following: "Do not let your hearts be troubled. Trust in God; trust also in me." I have been in the basement many times in my life, but God was always there when I needed Him. We must remember that if we never face trouble, then we will never need to call on Jesus.

Trouble can come in many forms and the enemy packages it in deceptive ways. Throughout history, even holy men of God have fallen, and many times they have succumbed to the wiles of beautiful but wicked women.

Back in the fall of 1996 we were contracted to remodel a structure, that was actually a 1930s filling station. Their desire was to turn the station into a home. It was a vast project because the station was in such bad shape. Back then we didn't have an ear to hear what the Holy Spirit was saying. We should have turned the job down but we didn't, and so it became another basement in the adventure of life.

We were roughly one or two days away from completely finishing the project, when we went to work one morning and found that the locks had been changed. I called the owner, who said we were fired because she was dissatisfied with our work. I immediately contacted our attorney and he filed a mechanic's lien on the property and then filed a lawsuit. When it was all said and done, a judge ruled against us and we have appealed it all the way to the Indiana Supreme Court. That basement experience has dragged out for the last five years, but God has been there with us every single step of the way and never failed us.

Jesus tells us in Matthew 5:11 and 12: "Blessed are you when people insult you; persecute you and falsely say all kinds of evil against you because of me. Rejoice and be glad, because great is your reward in heaven, for in the same way they persecuted the prophets who were before you." Proverbs 24:10 tells us, "If you falter in times of trouble, how small is your strength!" My experience with customers who wouldn't pay wasn't over, and I would need a great deal of spiritual strength to endure what was to come.

I really enjoy building new homes, because they give me a great deal of satisfaction and a feeling of accomplishment. Another young couple hired us to build them a new home. I could tell from the very first day that they were biting off more than they could chew, but I continued anyway. We finished our work in the fall of 1999, but the owner was so far in debt that he couldn't pay us to build the entire house, so he chose to do most of the work himself.

Everything seemed to go well until I sent a bill for the remaining amount due. The homeowner had his lawyer send me a letter, which stated that his client had damage to his home caused by defective workmanship. My attorney immediately filed a mechanic's lien, and we are still waiting to foreclose on the house.

In Indiana, the law states that a homeowner must let the contractor know any problems and give him the opportunity to correct them. If the homeowner doesn't allow that, they are in the wrong, but on the other hand, if the contractor refuses to correct the problem, he is in the wrong. That particular homeowner has admitted he doesn't have the money to pay us and has never told us what the problems are nor does he desire for us to fix them.

At that time, I wasn't a very good judge of character, because my walk with the Spirit was weak. I needed a greater gift of discernment than I had, and thankfully I do a much better job of walking in the Spirit now. You might say the fire tempered me while I lived in that basement called life.

Repaired and Back in Service

My faith is in the Lord now. Jesus tells us in Matthew 6:34: "Therefore do not worry about tomorrow, for tomorrow will worry about itself. Each day has enough trouble of its own." I like to compare mankind to household appliances. Parts on appliances break, but they can be fixed. After the appliance is repaired, it is put back into service. Similarly, parts of our lives often break down and the Lord repairs us, and then He puts us back into His service. You might say that God is a holy mechanic. When trouble comes, we want to give up and throw in the towel, but He says, "Wait a minute, I can fix that, now get back in there." When we think we've lost it all, that's the time to lean on the Lord the most.

I can't think of a deeper basement to be in than the one of mourning the loss of a child. There is a local couple we're friends with who recently lost a child. That couple owns the local convenience store, and the mother couldn't go to work for the first month or so. I spoke with the father shortly after that and all I could say was, "I'm sorry!" I must say the father seems to be holding up rather well, under the circumstances.

I told the father that one of two things would happen with him and his wife. I said they would both draw closer to the Lord and gain from His strength, or they would simply run away from Him. I will never forget what he told me. He said, "We're not running!"

That man told me of how God strengthened them shortly after the accident. An older couple that attends their church approached them and told them of their own loss. They too had lost a son and told our young friends that if they needed to talk, they could call any time. The older couple gave our young friends some comforting thoughts, and said, "Although you will never forget the loss, you will always have the joyful memories of them."

2 Corinthians 4:16-18 and 2 Corinthians 5:1 tells us this:

Therefore we do not lose heart. Though outwardly we are wasting away, yet inwardly we are being renewed day by day. For our light and momentary troubles are achieving for us an eternal glory that far outweighs them all. So we fix our eyes not on what is seen, but on what is unseen. For what is seen is temporary, but what is unseen is eternal. Now we know that if the earthly tent we live in is destroyed, we have a building from God, an eternal house in heaven, not built by human hands.

Nothing can describe the loss a woman feels when she miscarries a baby. It's a deep basement that no woman cares to dwell in, and a man can't even experience or understand the loss. The only man who can truly understand it is Jesus.

We recently built a room addition for a young couple that had lost a child. I noticed pictures of their deceased baby hanging on the wall of the hallway and some taped to toolboxes in the garage. There was another photo hanging on the wall that caught my eye. It was an image of their daughter standing in front of the baby's grave, holding a flower. When I looked at those photos I realized something. They loved their baby and they wanted to hold onto the lasting memory of that beautiful child.

After Cindy gave birth to Raine, we decided to try again, but she experienced two miscarriages after that. It was hard for us to understand why that happened, but we never stopped trying, and I'm so glad because God blessed us with Katie. Although both babies were only three or four months old when they died, I think of what they could have been.

I remember walking into the hospital room after my wife's second loss. I had a handful of flowers and had every intention of cheering her up. I found her staring out the window in silence, and I handed her the flowers. She placed them in the bedpan, and I knew at that moment that words would be useless. I sat in the chair beside her bed for what seemed like hours, and we both stared out the window together and mourned our loss.

Ladies, I know of no words that can describe this loss, but be assured that your lost child runs and plays without a care in the world because they are running into the loving arms of the Father. Your child is holding the Lord's hand, and they are waiting in earnest for your arrival. When that day comes, the Father and your baby will have tears of joy streaming down their faces. The Lord will release your child's hand and they will run into your arms and say, "I missed you, Mommy."

Your worst days are never so bad that you are beyond the reach of God's grace, and your best days are never so good that you are beyond the need of it. Jesus wants to leave you with these words, found in John 16:33: "I have told you these things, so that in me you may have peace. In this world you will have trouble. But take heart! I have overcome the world."

Chapter Eleven

Is Your Floor Bouncy?

The purpose of this chapter is to talk about the type of individual who lives on a spiritual roller coaster. They may be on fire for the Lord one week but they are sinning the next. 1Thessalonians 5:22 tells us to, "Avoid every kind of evil," but sin can be packaged in many forms. It can be large, it can be small, it can be obvious and it can also seem innocent. Sin, however, is always sin, and we are instructed to avoid it at all times. The Bible says that we live in the world but aren't of the world, and that's a message that most people overlook. They want to be labeled as a Christian, but they don't want to sacrifice their earthly lifestyle. Jesus tells us in Matthew 24:12 that "Because of the increase of wickedness, the love of most will grow cold."

This chapter will discuss floors and defects that can occur with them. Floors may sometimes need a little help, just like we do. In the construction industry, this is called shoring, and we all need a little shoring up from time to time. Like most of you, I find myself seeking constant support. If there's ever a spiritual defect in my life, I look to the Bible for support. If your life is sinking, shore it up with God's Word. Don't seek the world for your answers, seek the Lord and you won't regret it.

Once you have finished your foundation, it's time to construct the floor. When we are constructing a home and it comes time to order the material, we order the floor package. The floor package consists of floor joists and the sub-floor. The floor joist is the component of the floor system that supports the weight load by resting on top of the foundation walls.

Now let's talk a bit about floor defects. Have you ever walked on a floor or step that was squeaky? This problem generally exists when the wood shrinks and a small space develops between the sub-floor and the support under it. In other words, what you are stepping on isn't resting entirely on its support, and is sliding downward on the shaft of the nail. When you release your weight from the surface, the material slides upward on the nail, which causes the squeaking noise. That type of defect can easily be corrected, and we always glue and nail our sub-floors for that specific reason.

When someone says that your floor is bouncy, they are talking about deflection. "Deflection" is a term used to describe the side to side or up and down movement of a flooring system. Virtually all flooring systems have deflection, but the degrees vary as to how much of it you can feel.

Reasons For Godlessness

I often wonder why people do the evil things they do, and why is there such godlessness in the world today. We can find the answer to this question in 2 Timothy 3:1-5:

> *But mark this: There will be terrible times in the last days. People will be lovers of themselves, lovers of money, boastful, proud, abusive, disobedient to their parents, ungrateful, unholy, without love, unforgiving, slanderous, without self-control, brutal, not lovers of the good, treacherous, rash, conceited, lovers of pleasure rather than lovers of God-having a form of Godliness but denying its power.*

Verse 5 goes on to tell us to, "Have nothing to do with them!"

As I stated in the introduction of this chapter, we will study the behavior of those who live on a spiritual roller coaster. I compare this lifestyle to deflection of a floor. These people often deflect from side to side and up and down, and they can spring from being hot in their spiritual life to being depressed and cold.

Around a year ago, God used something so simple to illustrate this that it became a real topic of discussion at our church. I was standing in the lot next door when something told me to burn the scrap lumber that was lying on the burn pile. Raine saw what I was doing and asked, "Are you crazy? Dad, it's dry and windy out here, what do you think you're doing?"

I said, "Something told me to burn it, Raine."

She thought I was a nut, but the neighbor next door, who is a Baptist, saw the fire and brought over a load of branches. He asked me, "Can I burn these?"

I answered, "Sure!"

The spirit of the Lord came upon me while that fire was raging and said He wants to throw us on the fire. I immediately ran inside, called the pastor, and told him that the Lord wants to throw us on the fire. I really don't think he knew what the Lord was talking about at that time but he does now. The Lord has been throwing our entire church on the fire lately.

The next day came and it was Saturday. God told me to drive to the Lebanon Park and pray. I didn't know what I was praying for but the Lord did. After praying for what felt like hours, I decided to pick my daughter up, but the Lord had other plans.

As I drove past my mother's apartment complex, the Lord told me to pull into the driveway and gather up some withered branches, bundle them, and place a note on them that read, "John 15:5-6." I asked the Lord, "Where am I going to find withered branches? I will have to drive all over Lebanon. If I go up to someone's house and ask for their withered branches, they'll call the cops because they'll think I'm a nut!" That was not what God wanted to hear.

I parked my truck and walked upstairs to my mother's apartment. While I was standing outside her door knocking, I noticed a man across the parking lot trimming branches from a small tree. As my mom answered the door, I ran down the stairs, yelling, "He's got branches!" I walked across the parking lot and noticed that the man was a long time friend whom I knew from childhood. He had recently been saved and I told him what the Lord had required of me.

My friend had recently undergone lung transplant surgery, and I told him he had no business out in the hot sun cutting a tree down. He told me that he had promised his elderly neighbor he would remove the tree because it was growing into the side of her home. He went on to say that he had gotten up that morning and, although he hadn't felt very well, he had made a promise to his neighbor that he had to keep. I wouldn't hear of it, though, so I grabbed the saw from his hand and cut the tree down. We cleaned up the mess and he thanked me. As I was walking away, I saw an elderly lady come out of the home and hug my friend. She told him, "Thank you for helping me." That was a story in itself, but little did I realize that God wasn't finished yet.

The next day came, and it was time for Sunday school. The Lord told me to walk into the church and lay the withered branches on the altar. I thought about what John 15:5-6 said. It reads like this:

> *I am the vine; you are the branches. If a man remains in me and I in him, he will bear much fruit; apart from me you can do nothing. If anyone does not remain in me, he is like a branch that is thrown away and withers; such branches are picked up, thrown into the fire and burned.*

After reading those scriptures, I was determined to place

those dead branches on that altar, and nothing was going to stop me from completing my mission.

We arrived at the church a few minutes early. Cindy was too embarrassed to walk inside with me while I was holding the branches, so she stayed in the car. As soon as I walked through the front door, the man and woman who greet people pointed their fingers and asked, "What is that?"

I said, "It's God's will!"

The lady rolled her eyes, but the man looked at me and said, "Well, praise God then!"

As I walked to the front of the church, I felt all eyes watching me. I laid the branches on the altar like the Lord had instructed, took my seat, and observed the spirit of indifference and pride in action. The worship team leader stared at the branches and said, "Hey boys, look! Instead of bringing us roses, the pastor brought us weeds!" The choir leader saw the branches and stared down his nose at them through his reading glasses. Every single choir member that walked past the branches looked at them, but no one, absolutely no one, grabbed their Bible to look up the verses.

I got the pastor's attention before the service and told him of my actions, but he told me that he needed to lay them to the side so he could teach his class. I never heard another word about those branches again. You may think that was the end of the story but the Lord wasn't finished yet.

The next day, the Lord told me to leave a message with the pastor's secretary. The message was this: 1 Corinthians 1:27. "God chose the foolish things of the world to shame the wise; God chose the weak things of the world to shame the strong." Dead branches on the altar seemed quite foolish to the majority of people that Sunday, so I thought that would be the end of the dead branch experience.

About a month later, one of the assistant pastors asked me about the branches and what they had meant. When I told him it was God's will, he asked me where the branches were. I told him that they were behind the stage, as far as I knew. I would later find out that both youth leaders found the branches in that same spot and talked to the pastor about them. Both of them asked the pastor what he planned to do with them, and he said, "Nothing." One of those pastors teaches a junior high class, and the other teaches a high school class. Both of them were able to use those branches to lead young people to the Lord. Praise God for dead branches!

Revealing His Purposes

There are times in our lives when God sweeps away the dirt of the world to reveal His purpose. Shortly before I began to write this book, the Lord said He would unfold His plan for my life in front of my eyes. I pray that the plan may be a writing ministry, but my true desire is to only serve the Lord. Pray that the glory of the Lord will rest on the words contained in this book and pray for the author while you're at it! I don't want to be "bouncy." I desire to write with fire, so help me spread that fire to God's people.

Remember that story, "The Christmas Carol?" If you recall, Scrooge's partner died and his ghost came back to haunt him. That ghost was weighed down with chains, and the chains in your life can be heavy ones too, if you let them. A friend recently shared something with me that I thought was interesting. There are times when Satan will use your past against you. That particular lady was weighing herself down with guilt, and she felt like she could have done more for her husband before he passed away. I told her, "Satan's the master of guilt and he's using it against you."

Satan would love to wrap the chains of guilt around your neck and suffocate you with them, but remember what God said about him. He comes to steal, kill, and destroy. Are you tired of dragging those heavy chains around? Jesus can break those chains if you'll give Him a chance. 1 Thessalonians 5:16-18 shows us the way. It says, "Be joyful always; pray continually; give thanks in all circumstances, for this is God's will for you in Christ Jesus."

Breaking Habits

While we're on the subject of breaking things, I'd like to talk about breaking habits. Some habits are very hard to break while some are rather easy, but I assure you that there is virtually no habit that we can't break with the Lord's assistance. All we have to do is ask.

We need to express patience with those who are struggling with bad habits. They didn't develop those habits overnight, and they may not be able to extinguish them immediately. It may take Jesus a little while to saw through their chains.

While attending one church, the Lord spoke to me and suggested that I convey His message to one of the members. I walked over to a couple and told the wife what the Lord had said. I told her, "What may seem silly or foolish to others isn't foolish to God." I now know what 1 Corinthians 1:27 says, but I didn't back then. The woman's husband looked at me in amazement, and she told me she was working on something at the time, but I never found out what it was. That wouldn't be the last time the Lord would speak to her.

Shortly after that encounter, the couple asked if we could haul them some gravel for their driveway, and I said, "Of course, for a small fee." I drove our large dump truck to the gravel pit that Saturday, and I can't remember exactly how much weight we had on that truck, but I think it was 10 or 15 tons. God is always looking out for His children, and He sure had His hand of protection on us that day.

I knew we had a lot of weight on the truck so I was driving slowly, when suddenly we had a rear tire blowout. I was literally all over the road, and Randie began screaming. I remember saying, "Help me, Lord" under my breath! I finally got the truck under control and pulled to the side of the road, and guess who just happened to be behind me to witness the entire event? A driver who worked for a tire service company was driving right behind me. He said that the right rear inside dual tire had blown out. The force of that blowout had knocked the right outside dual tire completely off its rim. He asked, "Are you and the girl alright?"

I said, "Yes, just a little nervous and scared is all."

The man said he was a Christian and that he wanted to help us, so I let him. He removed the tires from the truck, drove us to town, got them repaired, and drove us back out to the truck to install them. I tried to pay him, but he wouldn't let me. We already had a full day of excitement and it wasn't even ten o'clock in the morning yet. We still had gravel to deliver.

When we arrived at the couple's house, I told the wife what happened, and she was extremely glad that we were okay. We unloaded the gravel and she invited us inside for something to drink. I can't remember what we were talking about in her kitchen but suddenly, the Spirit told me to tell her something. I said, "Gail, the Lord has something He wants to tell you."

She said, "What is it?"

I told her that He said, "Let Me rain on you."

Everyone in that house, including me, was surprised by her response. She began crying and showed no signs of stopping. I just sat there at her kitchen table and enjoyed watching the Lord pour His glory onto her. Eventually, I told Randie that it was time to go, and Gail's son and daughter looked at me in a strange silence. They weren't saying a word, but I had a pretty good idea what they were thinking. They wanted to know what I had done to their mom.

Her husband cornered me the next day during Sunday school and asked, "What in the world did you do to my wife? You left at one o'clock in the afternoon and she was still crying at ten o'clock that night when I got home!"

I told him, "I didn't do anything! It was the Lord who decided to sprinkle his cleansing spirit on her yesterday."

I think every marriage needs cleansing from time to time. My marriage has been bouncy from time to time. It's been that way for almost 20 years, and I'm sure that some of you can relate to that. Families are built on love and Satan hates that. The family is the basic element of all civilizations, and if Satan can destroy it, he's accomplished his goal. Don't let it happen!

Chapter Twelve

Up Go the Walls!

Now that we have finished with the floor, it's time to put up the walls. Many customers have told me that when the walls start going up they can finally begin to envision what the structure will look like. That's when the house really starts to look like something.

The term used to describe wall construction is "framing," and there are various ways to frame a structure. Framing techniques vary from contractor to contractor. A famous quote of mine is, "Talk to ten different people, and you'll get ten different opinions." The same holds true for technique, because every contractor has a different one. Each contractor has the same goal in mind, but they use a different technique to accomplish it. God works in the same manner. He uses different people under different circumstances to accomplish His goal. God's ultimate goal is that none should perish without knowing Him.

Once the walls of your house are finished, it's time for insulation. There are several different types of insulation, but we will focus on the two most common ones: roll fiberglass and the blown-in type. Roll fiberglass insulation comes in many different sizes, and the R factor, which describes its resistance to heat loss, rates its insulating power. Roll fiberglass insulation typically comes in 15" or 23" wide rolls, and the higher the R factor, the thicker the insulation.

Now let's talk about the blown-in type insulation. A popular type of blown-in insulation is cellulose, which is actually finely ground newspaper with a fireproof chemical added. Blown-in insulation is also rated by R factor, and the thicker it is, the higher the R factor. Code requirements for insulation vary from state to state because of climate. I can tell you that homes in Indiana are required to have R-38 in the attic, which requires 13" of cellulose blown-in insulation.

Walls of Separation

I'm interested in the type of people who insulate themselves from the world. People, and sometimes even nations, will build walls of separation. The basic physical type of wall that comes to mind is a neighbor's fence, but there are historical walls as well. Consider the walls of Jericho, Berlin, and China.

In addition to building physical walls and fences to keep others out, people also erect mental ones. This chapter is really about those who insulate themselves and the mental walls they use to block others out. Peter gives us some great advice in 1 Peter 4:8-10.

> *Above all, love each other deeply, because love covers a multitude of sins. Offer hospitality to one another without grumbling. Each one should use whatever gift he has received to serve others, faithfully administering God's grace in its various forms.*

In a roundabout way, Peter was saying, "I don't have to attend every argument that I'm invited to!"

I'd like to tell you about someone who had a hard head, loved to argue, and could build a mental wall as strong as anyone's. Grandma Wilcox, my mom's mom, was a powerful woman of God, but she had her faults as we all do. The main thing I remember about her was that she had a head of granite and a will to match. If she formed an opinion about someone or something, nothing was going to change her mind about it.

I'm convinced that putting up walls isn't in God's divine plan. Romans 12:13 tells us to "Share with God's people who are in need. Practice hospitality." Webster's dictionary defines "hospitable" as, "Favorably receptive or open." Loving others, and being receptive and open, is the type of behavior that God is looking for, but being stubborn and hard to get along with isn't quite what He has in mind. Building a wall to insulate yourself from the world definitely isn't the way to go.

I can remember discussing the meaning of a particular word with Grandma once. I was pretty confident that it was defined a particular way, but Grandma felt differently. I found out that I was right about the definition and I showed her what the dictionary said about it, but that didn't seem to matter to her. Our conversation then became heated. I can still remember what she said to this day. She said, "I don't care what Funk and Wagnall says."

Proverbs 18:1-2 tells us this: "An unfriendly man pursues selfish ends; he defies all sound judgment. A fool finds no pleasure in understanding but delights in airing his own opinions." I would never say that my grandmother was a fool, but she could have been a little more understanding at times.

Romans 2:5 says, "Because of your stubbornness and your unrepentant heart, you are storing up wrath against yourself for the day of God's wrath, when his righteous judgment will be revealed." Don't get me wrong, I don't think Grandma sinned in her stubborn ways, but it really wasn't God's best for her either.

Have you ever tried to figure out what someone from the past might have been thinking during a historical event? When Cindy and I visited Gettysburg, Pennsylvania on our vacation two years ago, we were quite moved by the written statements made by the soldiers who were involved in that battle. I tried to picture in my mind what the horror of battle might have been like on that day. Thousands of men lost their lives in that three-day battle, and the battlefield stretched for miles. As we drove along the tour route, we read many of the plaques, and several of the soldier's quotes mentioned prayer.

On the last day of the battle, the South decided to charge, and they formed a human wall ten men deep and over a mile wide. The North was beaten up badly, but they still managed to hold their ground and the South eventually retreated. Over 50,000 men lost their lives during that three-day battle. I tried to envision the sight in my mind and the thousands of men who were asking the Lord to forgive them of their sins before they died.

The truly sad part about the Civil War was that people built walls between each other over slavery. Brother fought against brother during that war, and I think 1 Peter 2:15-17 had something to say to the people of the 1860s, but some chose to listen and some didn't.

For it is God's will that by doing good you should silence the ignorant talk of foolish men. Live as free men, but do not use your freedom as a cover-up for evil; live as servants of God. Show proper respect to everyone: love the brotherhood of believers, fear God, honor the king.

God Will Sustain Us

There are certain individuals who shake their fist in the air and yell at God when trouble comes their way. First of all, let me say that type of behavior can be very dangerous. Never tempt God out of anger because you may regret it. I'm convinced that those who behave that way have had something happen to them in their past and they blame God for it. Instead of blaming God, they should do what Psalms 55:22 says: "Cast your cares on the Lord and he will sustain you; he will never let the righteous fall." Take some good advice. Forge on, don't give up and don't isolate yourself. If it's been your habit in the past to throw up walls, maybe it's time to hand Jesus a hammer and chisel and let Him start chipping away at the problem!

Remember the Unabomber? He's an excellent example of someone who lived in isolation and rejected society. He was an intelligent man who hated authority, and so he mailed several bombs that killed people. It took the authorities nearly 20 years to catch him, and his brother was the one who eventually turned him in. Some people build walls and they eventually act on that emotion. Ted Kascinski acted on his emotions, and he's going to live in prison for the rest of his life because of it.

Take Down the Walls

Have you ever heard of someone being called a bigot? Webster's dictionary defines "bigot" as "A person who is extremely intolerant of another's creed, belief, or opinion."

Deuteronomy 15:7 tells us this: "If there is a poor man among your brothers in any of the towns of the land that the Lord your God is giving you, do not be hardhearted or tightfisted toward your poor brother." Romans 12:16 instructs us to "Live in harmony with one another. Do not be proud, but be willing to associate with people of low position. Do not be conceited."

To be honest with you, I was a bigot myself. I used to look down on mixed marriages and had the opinion that people should marry only within their own race, but I no longer feel that way. I changed my mind when the Lord convinced me that everyone is His child. Skin color makes no difference to Him because He looks at the heart.

If you have walls in your life, it's time to take them apart. Just because you have been raised with a certain opinion that doesn't mean it's the truth. Walls don't have to be permanent structures if you desire their removal.

Before you can change your mind you have to change your heart. The Lord is opening my eyes to the opinions of the heart. I believe that what's in your heart will eventually come out your mouth. Walls can mean virtually anything to anyone, but the love of God can conquer them all. Some of you have walls in your life and some of them have been there for quite some time. The Lord says, "The winds of change are coming, and it's time to renew your mind!"

About a month before Cindy's mom died, I drove her to the airport. She was taking a plane to visit her son in Arizona. As we were driving down the interstate I asked, "Mom, have you ever asked Jesus to come into your heart?" She said that she didn't believe in salvation. I said, "If salvation wasn't necessary, then Jesus died on the cross for absolutely no reason at all!" I had no idea that her last day on earth would be less than a month away, but asked her if she wanted Jesus to come into her life. She said, "No, thanks." She didn't take Jesus up on his offer. Matthew 7:7 says to "Ask and it will be given to you; seek and you will find; knock and the door will be opened to you." My mother-in-law locked the door to her heart, and she later died alone in her living room. I hope and pray that she remembered our conversation about Jesus, but only she and He know if she made the decision to accept him before she took her last breath. It has always been the hope of her loved ones that she did.

First John 1:8-10 clearly tells us why it's so dangerous to build walls in our heart.

If we claim to be without sin, we deceive ourselves and the truth is not in us. If we confess our sins, he is faithful and just and will forgive us our sins and purify us from all unrighteousness. If we claim we have not sinned, we make him out to be a liar and his word has no place in our lives.

People often say, "I can't change," but that's not true. You can teach an old dog new tricks, and with the help of the Holy Spirit you can change. Some of you have grown cold and indifferent, and you have a heart full of ice, but if you knew the Lord at one time and you've walked away from Him, it's not too late to reverse those thoughts. The Lord will take you back! Jeremiah 14:7 says, "Although our sins testify against us, O Lord, do something for the sake of your name. For our backsliding is great; we have sinned against you."

Perhaps something in your life has caused you to walk away from God, but I want you to realize something: It wasn't the Lord's decision to walk away from the relationship, it was yours! Satan used a circumstance or situation in your life to build a wall between you and Christ. What was it that persuaded you to walk away from the Lord? It doesn't matter if you can't remember, but now is the time for change. You have been living with that wall long enough.

Now I want to talk to those of you who have never asked the Lord to be your Savior. Jesus said in John 3:16 that, "For God so loved the world that he gave his one and only son, that whoever believes in him shall not perish but have eternal life." Jesus knew that His destiny would be death, but He died willingly for us. There is virtually no wall that can separate us from the love of God! His love is always present, we just need to recognize it and break the routine of the world. The Lord can change your life and He can change your mind, but you need to ask. Don't let anyone or anything tell you that you can't change. Seek the Lord for understanding, but most of all, seek Him for change!

CHAPTER THIRTEEN

How's Your Roof?

One thing that I have found about construction is that it is a lot like life—it's a building process. We build many things along the path of life. We build friendships, families, our faith, and most of all, integrity. It's my goal in this chapter to make you realize what's really important in life. Everyone thinks a roof over their head is extremely important because no one desires to be homeless, but building a Christian life full of integrity is even more important.

Since the walls are now complete, it's time to frame the roof. Every roof is different, and each one consists of many different components. Some roofs are easy to frame while others are quite difficult. In the 1950s, many builders began constructing homes that were called "ranch style," and it's not uncommon to see them still being built today. The roof on that type of house is pretty basic and is called a gable roof..

The roofs on many of today's deluxe style homes can be quite complicated to frame. That type of roof can have many angles, different pitches, and even different types of framing all incorporated into one roof. Much like life, that type of roof can really be a challenge to build.

Now that we have our roof framed, it's time to install the

shingles. Shingles are a roof covering that can be made of asphalt, fiberglass, wood, tile, slate, or any other material or combination thereof. Shingles also come in many different styles, colors, and sizes. The steeper the pitch is on a roof, the faster the water will run off and therefore, the longer the shingles will last. If the roof pitch is low, the shingles will wear out faster because the water stands longer.

I don't know about you, but just thinking about all that work has made me tired. It's my desire to help you understand the construction of your roof and not to confuse you. I hope you're beginning to see the similarity between your Christian walk and a roof. They both consist of many things and, although they can be a lot of work to construct, they are quite important to us all.

As I said before, the purpose of this chapter is to make you think about what is important in your life. Do your priorities mirror God's priorities? Colossians 3:2 says to "Set your minds on things above, not on earthly things." Verse 5 says to "Put to death, therefore, whatever belongs to your earthly nature: sexual immorality, impurity, lust, evil desires and greed, which is idolatry." Verses 7 and 8 go on to say "You used to walk in these ways, in the life you once lived. But now you must rid yourselves of all such things as these: anger, rage, malice, slander, and filthy language from your lips."

Jesus tells us in Matthew 22:37-39 to "Love the Lord your God with all your heart and with all your soul and with all your mind. This is the first and greatest commandment. And the second is: Love your neighbor as yourself." I'm about to throw a series of questions at you, and I want you to give them some serious thought.

When you look up, what do you see above you? The ceiling? The stars? How about the love of God? Joshua 22:5 says to be "Very careful to keep the commandment and the law that Moses the servant of the Lord gave you: to love the Lord your God, to walk in all his ways, to obey his commands, to hold fast to him and to serve him with all your heart and all your soul." Joshua publicly spoke of his own willingness to serve God when he said, "Choose for yourselves this day whom you will serve. But as for me and my household, we will serve the Lord" (Joshua 24:15). Who do you look up to? People that are taller than you? How about your heavenly Father?

What type of role model are you looking for? Parents? Professional athletes? Hollywood actors? The best role model you could ever choose would be Jesus. His brother James has some pretty good insight as to the good and bad characteristics of a role model:

> *Who is wise and understanding among you? Let him show it by his good life, by deeds done in the humility that comes from wisdom. But if you harbor bitter envy and selfish ambition in your hearts, do not boast about it or deny the truth. Such "wisdom" does not come down from heaven but is earthly, unspiritual, of the devil. For where you have envy and selfish ambition, there you find disorder and every evil practice* (James 3:13-16).

Jeremiah 10:23 says, "I know, O Lord, that a man's life is not his own; it is not for man to direct his steps." That was Jeremiah's prayer, and it's also mine. It's important to me when God directs my steps. Do you want Him to direct yours?

Who's your hero? If you had to think about that question, something's wrong. You should have responded instantly to that question without even giving it a second thought. Webster's dictionary defines "hero" as, "A man of distinguished courage or ability, admired for his brave deeds and noble qualities. An individual possessing godlike prowess and beneficence who often came to be honored as a divinity." Folks, there's only one true hero, He stands head and shoulders above everyone else, and His name is Jesus.

Colossians 3:20 says, "Children, obey your parents in everything, for this pleases the Lord," and Ephesians 6:1 says the exact same thing. Kids, if God didn't think it was important for you to obey your parents, He wouldn't have made a point of saying it twice, would He? I can assure you that God isn't pleased when you rebel against your parents. Satan rebelled against God and look what happened to him. The only exception to this rule is if your parents ask you to sin. Parents should never put their kids in a position to sin. Kids, if a parent asks you to sin, you have the right to tell them no. You should say, "Mom, Dad, please don't ask me to do that because it's a sin and God will judge me for it." Love your parents, kids, and have patience with them. They're far from perfect and they make mistakes just like you do. Here's something I'd like for you to think about. Are you proud of your parents (Proverbs 17:6)?

Parents, you have to earn the respect of your kids, and you can do so by treating them like decent human beings. If they're teenagers, try to treat them like adults. They resent being treated like kids when they're that age. Moms and dads should tell their kids they love them everyday. Don't ever think you're unloved or fatherless because you aren't. If your father is dead or just not around, read 2 Corinthians 6:18. "The Lord Almighty says, 'I will be a Father to you, and you will be my sons and daughters.'"

My wife Cindy got pregnant when she was in the Army, and the father of her baby asked her, "What are you going to do?" Cindy said, "I'm going to have the baby and I don't feel like getting married to you." I thank God she didn't abort Randie. I have told Randie several times that she is free to search after her biological father if she so desires, but she said she has thought about it before and has no desire to look him up. She tells me that I'm her dad. She feels that since her biological dad has never bothered to look her up or call, he has no interest in her. I love Randie and her heavenly Father loves her too. Who could ask for anything more?

Are you looking for your real dad? Pray about it, because you could be disappointed with what you find. The relationship you have with your adopted father or your step-dad may be a whole lot better than what you may find. I'm totally convinced that men and women can love children that aren't really their own flesh and blood. I'm talking about stepparents, foster parents, and parents who adopt.

Raine's boyfriend recently called me and asked me to pray for him. After he explained his situation to me I prayed for love and peace to manifest in his life. Before I hung the phone up I told him that I loved him and that I appreciated his kind spirit.

Raine's boyfriend comes from a broken home, and he asked me to pray for him because he was discouraged. Raine's boyfriend is a child of God, and he may or may not realize it, but more people than he thinks love him. Raine loves him, I love him, and Jesus loves him. The love of God is more than he can comprehend.

The bottom line is that we are either children of God or Satan. Listen to what Jesus had to say about fathers in John 8:42-47.

If God were your Father, you would love me, for I came from God and now I'm here. I have not come on my own; but he sent me. Why is my language not clear to you? Because you are unable to hear what I say. You belong to your father, the devil, and you want to carry out your father's desire. He was a murderer from the beginning, not holding to the truth, for there is no truth in him. When he lies, he speaks his native language, for he is a liar and the father of lies. Yet because I tell the truth, you do not believe me! Can any of you prove me guilty of sin? If I am telling the truth, why don't you believe me? He who belongs to God hears what God says. The reason you do not hear is that you do not belong to God.

Are you serving the father of lies or the father of truth? Satan is not only the father of lies, but he's also the master of guilt, depression, and low self-esteem. He loves to hang those kinds of feelings over your head. That's not the type of roof I desire to live under. Satan's true agenda for your life is death. He would love for you to commit suicide. Jesus said in John 10:10 that "The thief comes only to steal and kill and destroy; I have come that they may have life, and have it to the full."

Satan will use anything he can to claim your soul, and it's always by deceptive means. He deceives many people in many ways, but he deceives homosexuals by making them think they are just living an alternative lifestyle. Believe me, God created man and woman for a reason. If being a homosexual was God's plan, there wouldn't be any children, now would there?

Much like in the days of Noah, many people today are choosing the broad road that leads to the wide gate of destruction. Noah's life was an interesting one and I encourage you to read about him. The story of Noah's life starts at Genesis 5:28. Noah would need a solid roof over his head, not only to protect his family, but also God's creatures. I'd like to share with you a few tips that I learned from Noah.

#1 Don't miss the boat.

#2 Try to remember that we're all in the same boat.

#3 Plan ahead. It wasn't raining when Noah built the ark.

#4 Stay fit. When you're 600 years old, someone might ask you to do something REALLY big.

#5 Don't listen to the critics. Just get on with what has to be done.

#6 Two heads are better than one.

#7 When you're stressed, try floating for awhile.

#8 Remember that the ark was built by amateurs. It was the Titanic that was built by professionals.

#9 Remember that woodpeckers inside are a larger threat than storms outside.

#10 No matter what the difficulty, trust in the Lord. There'll be a rainbow at the end of the storm.

While we're talking about roofs, I've got a story I'd like to share with you. We were contacted to repair a roof in a neighboring town a few years back. The roof had literally leaked for years, and there was a hole roughly three or four feet in diameter that went through the floor, the ceiling, the attic, and through the roof. When you stood inside the room and looked upward, you could actually see the sky. The home was a rental property and the landlord discovered the damage when the tenant finally moved out. We repaired all the damage, but the sad part was that the tenant lived that way for years and didn't care. Some people take little or no pride in the way they live, but we must protect everything with which God blesses us.

I received a call from a lady from our church a few years ago. She was reading about the armor of God in Ephesians and had a question about the helmet of salvation. Her question was, "What is the helmet for?" There are times when I don't know answers, but I always wait on the Lord for the answer and He generally gives it. I told the lady that the helmet of salvation was to protect her mind. Romans 12:2 says,

"Do not conform any longer to the pattern of this world, but be transformed by the renewing of your mind. Then you will be able to test and approve what God's will is-his good, pleasing and perfect will."

Psalms 26:2 says to "Test me, O Lord, and try me, examine my heart and my mind." Your mind is the roof that covers your soul, so protect it. If you allow the things of the world to leak into your spirit, they will cause eternal damage. I would like to end the discussion with a thought and a scripture. The thought is this: "Your attitude is the conditioning of your mind!" Paul gives us some wise tips on how to condition our minds in Philippians 2:3-5. "Do nothing out of selfish ambition or vain conceit, but in humility consider others better than yourselves. Each of you should look not only to your own interests, but also to the interests of others. Your attitude should be the same as that of Christ Jesus."

CHAPTER FOURTEEN

Short-Circuiting God's Will

This chapter will cover the three basic elements that are needed in a home—plumbing, electricity, and heating and cooling. It would be safe to say that most Americans don't realize how much they rely on these elements until they need repair. Our spiritual life is also much like that. We don't realize how blessed we are until the bottom falls out and trouble comes. God desires the best for his people, but we get in His way sometimes and short-circuit His will.

1 John 5:14,15 says, "This is the confidence we have in approaching God: That if we ask anything according to his will, he hears us. And if we know that he hears us—whatever we ask—we know that we have what we asked of him." We are also told in Ephesians 5:17 to "Therefore, do not be foolish, but understand what the Lord's will is." I can't stress enough how important it is to do God's will. Things don't run smoothly when we're out of His will.

Let's talk about the mechanical features of your home and start with plumbing. Plumbing features water supply and waste removal, both of which are very important. Your body is made up of 70% water and you can't go very long without it. HVAC is a common term that is used in the construction field today and its initials stand for Heating, Ventilation and Air-Conditioning. The heating and cooling systems of today are very complicated and take years of education to master. The world of HVAC can really be a complicated one. And last, but not least, there's electricity. Electricity is crucial to most of us because everything, and I mean everything, runs off of it these days.

Remember when I talked about framing in chapter 12? I said that no two contractors frame the same. They do the job correctly with the same goal in mind, but they take different paths to reach that goal. I also compared that to your spiritual walk with Christ and said that we all have the same goal in mind but that God sends us down different paths to reach it. Plumbers, electricians, and HVAC technicians are no different. They may not all do the job in the same manner, but they have the same goal in mind.

As you may already know, there are local, and in some cases, state laws, known as "codes," that mandate what wiring materials you can use in your home and how they're to be installed. Ignoring those statutes not only risks a fine and an order to do the work over again, but it also jeopardizes the safety of the inhabitants.

If you're planning to extend an existing circuit or add a new one, you may need to apply for a permit and arrange to have the work inspected before it's put into service. Local officials can tell you about that and whether or not you'll need a licensed electrician to "sign-off" on the job.

Jesus said in John 8:12 that "I am the light of the world. Whoever follows me will never walk in darkness, but will have the light of life." You can turn electricity off or on anytime you want and some of you think you can do that to God. My best advice to you is to leave the spiritual light on. 2 Corinthians 4:6 says, "For God, who said, 'Let light shine out of darkness,' made his light shine in our hearts to give us the light of the knowledge of the glory of God in the face of Christ." Think about that scripture for a minute, and let it sink in.

Psalms 143:10 says, "Teach me to do your will, for you are my God; may your good spirit lead me on level ground." Inject God's Word into your life instead of letting it collect dust on the shelf. It's time to blow the dust off and be about the Father's business because the world is short-circuiting. You can watch the news on any given night and discover that for yourself.

America has been attacked, and we now have troops in the Middle East. These are some uncertain times that we live in, my friend, but rest assured that there is no need to fear the future. Amos 5:13,14 says, "Therefore the prudent man keeps quiet in such times, for the times are evil. Seek good, not evil, that you may live. Then the Lord God Almighty will be with you, just as you say he is." Some are asking if we are close to the end of time, and I would say that we're close. That's why you need to be prepared. If your life's not right with the Lord, you need to make it right.

I'm convinced that the Church will witness the greatest revival that the world has ever seen before Jesus returns. The church in America has been too relaxed for too long, but all that is about to change. The Lord told me "The winds of change are coming!" My mom said she's heard other ministers say the exact same thing on television, and that's no coincidence. That's the Holy Spirit talking! We all need to be mindful of God's will, and we also need to be very cautious so as to not short-circuit His divine plan.

I want to tell you something. On any given day God's plan for our lives can change. Circumstances are different in the lives of His people every week, and that's why the Holy Spirit moves differently in each church service. When we get into the habit of doing the same old thing each week, we short-circuit His will for us. We should take Isaiah's advice and throw our tradition out the window. He says in Isaiah 43:18 to "Forget the former things; do not dwell on the past."

Psalms 62:8 says to, "Trust in him at all times, O people; pour out your hearts to him, for God is our refuge." My church is starting to do that very thing, and I'm seeing a change in the people and a hunger for God that I didn't see before. If you want change in your life, let Psalms 40:8 be your personal prayer. It's mine.

Listening to the Holy Spirit

I feel that some of you are afraid of what the Holy Spirit might do in your life because you fear change. The Holy Spirit comes to convict and instruct us about life, and we should never fear it. I can't stress enough how important it is to listen to God's will for us through the Holy Spirit. I'm going to give you a group of seven scriptures to think about, and to emphasize the point I'm trying to make.

Here's what Jesus had to say about the Holy Spirit in John 16:8-11:

When he goes, he will convict the world of guilt in regard to sin and righteousness and judgment: In regard to sin, because men do not believe in me; in regard to righteousness, because I am going to the Father, where you can see me no longer; and in regard to judgment, because the prince of this world now stands condemned.

Look at what Jesus promised us in John 14:26,27:

The Counselor, the Holy Spirit, whom the Father will send in my name, will teach you all things and will remind you of everything I have said to you. Peace I leave with you; my peace I give you. I do not give to you as the world gives. Do not let your hearts be troubled and do not be afraid.

Psalms 32:8 says, "I will instruct you and teach you in the way you should go; I will counsel you and watch over you."

Proverbs 8:33,34 tells us to "Listen to my instruction and be wise; do not ignore it. Blessed is the man who listens to me, watching daily at my doors, waiting at my doorway."

Proverbs 4:13 tells us to "Hold on to instruction, do not let it go; guard it well, for it is your life."

Proverbs 19:20 says to "Listen to advise and accept instruction, and in the end you will be wise."

Jesus sums up my point by saying this in Matthew 5:6: "Blessed are those who hunger and thirst for righteousness, for they will be filled." I have a constant hunger and thirst for the things of the Lord, and I have no desire to stop the flow of blessings that He has for my life. It's my humble prayer that you're beginning to understand how important it is to listen to the instruction of the Holy Spirit. If we don't, we will short-circuit the plan He has for us.

There's a spiritual war going on over your soul. I compare it to the battles that were waged on the high seas in the days of the ironclad ships. The Lord sails in a white ship while Satan sails in his, and the circumstances of life come in the form of cannon fire. God launches a volley of blessings, and Satan immediately retaliates by launching his nasty volley.

It's also important to remember that Satan is always trying to imitate what God does. Satan will aim his cannon at the same area of your life that God does, but don't be deceived by that. He doesn't have your well being in mind like God does. Jesus tells us this in Matthew 10:28:

> *Do not be afraid of those who kill the body but cannot kill the soul. Rather, be afraid of the one who can destroy both soul and body in hell.*

The story I'm about to share with you emphasizes the importance of listening to the Holy Spirit. This shows what would have happened if my friend hadn't listened to what the Holy Spirit had to say. He would not only have short-circuited a man's life, but he would have also short-circuited God's plan for that man's life.

My friend told me that there were a rash of robberies in our area back in the early 70s, and all of the police departments in the surrounding counties knew who was committing them. My friend said the man was a smart criminal and a dangerous one too. The man was considered a famous cat burglar, and my friend said that most police departments were afraid of him.

He was the police chief at the time when his department cornered the cat burglar in a building . He had his pistol drawn and was aiming it when the cat burglar walked into his sights. My friend said the Holy Spirit immediately said "Don't shoot," and he lowered his weapon and placed it in its holster. The burglar was later captured alive and spent a short time in jail.

My friend told me that the former cat burglar walked into our church one morning and gave his heart to the Lord. He still comes to our church once in a while and is living a normal life in that town. Proverbs 16:20 says, "Whoever gives heed to instruction prospers, and blessed is he who trusts in the Lord." Thank God my friend listened and didn't kill that man. God had a divine plan for that cat burglar's life.

Jesus said in Acts 20:35 that "It is more blessed to give than to receive." Do you know someone you try to bless but they simply won't accept it? Rejecting the blessings of God can be dangerous because if you pour them out you may allow curses to come in. I believe that pride is the number one reason why people do things like that.

Have you ever asked yourself the question, "What's important to God?" It's not money, and it's not the things of this world. He cares about his children. Listen to what Jesus had to say in Matthew 18:12-14.

What do you think? If a man owns a hundred sheep, and one of them wanders away, will he not leave the ninety-nine on the hills and go to look for the one that wandered off? And if he finds it, I tell you the truth, he is happier about that one sheep than about the ninety-nine that did not wander off. In the same way your Father in heaven is not willing that any of these little ones should be lost.

Are you starting to see God's will yet? I'll leave you with this thought that's found in Proverbs 11:30. "The fruit of the righteous is a tree of life, and he who wins souls is wise."

CHAPTER FIFTEEN

Viewing the World

I would guess that the development of the earliest door probably came when someone decided to place an animal skin over the opening of their cave to keep the wind out, and the first window was probably just a hole in the wall. The technology used in making doors and windows has come a long way since then.

Let's talk about windows. There are five basic window types, of which the double-hung is the most popular. Then there are window sizes. The manufacturer that we purchase our windows from produces over six thousand different sizes. The windows of today are far more energy efficient than those of the past. Top-of-the-line windows are made with double or even triple pane glass construction. A double pane window is far more efficient than a single pane unit. Today's doors are also energy efficient. They are generally made of wood, fiberglass, or metal, and pre-hung units are by far the most popular because of the ease of installation.

Jesus had some rather deep and interesting things to say about doors in Revelation 3:19-22. He said:

Those who I love I rebuke and discipline. So be

earnest, and repent. Here I am! I stand at the door
and knock. If anyone hears my voice and opens the
door, I will come in and eat with him, and he with
me. To him who overcomes, I will give the right to sit
with me on my throne, just as I overcame and sat
down with my Father on his throne. He who has an
ear, let him hear what the Spirit says to the churches.

At one time, I felt like God was calling me to the ministry. After that, I felt like He called me to be a builder, and now I feel like He's calling me to be a writer. To be quite honest, I believe he's calling me to be all three of those. I'm building spirits while ministering His Word on these pages.

When you sit and watch your television set do you have a spirit of hope or a spirit of fear? The view of the world at present isn't a pretty one. America is in a financial recession and we are at war. Hundreds of thousands of Americans are losing their jobs and the seventh largest corporation in the world recently filed bankruptcy. More than 20,000 employees of that company not only lost their jobs, but they lost their entire retirement savings as well. I would say that they were left with nothing, but that wouldn't be entirely true. They do have someone to turn to, and that's God. I feel that God is allowing our present situations to occur so we will turn back to Him.

Many people are asking why terrorists would want to destroy us, and the simple answer is that they hate Israel and we are allies with Israel. That makes us their enemy. If America turns its back on Israel, then God will turn His back on us.

Things in the Middle East are now coming to a head. The Battle of Armageddon will take place in the Middle East just as the book of Revelation describes, and it will truly be World War III because all of the nations of the world will be involved. A large majority of the world's population will be killed in that war, and it will take months to bury the dead. President Bush is even describing our current war on terrorism as a battle of good versus evil.

We all know that our days on this earth are numbered, but

it's how we prepare for our final day that counts. I'd like to share the life story of one of my previous customers with you. Henry was an elderly black man who knew his future was short but didn't fear it. In fact, he was one of the bravest men I have ever known. I met him in 1998, when he hired a local Indianapolis contractor to repair the roof on his house. That contractor subcontracted the work to us. I don't normally accept subcontract work but something in my spirit told me to take that job.

Henry never viewed me as a white man, but rather as a Christian brother that he loved, and I respected him for that. We constantly stereotype people and things, but that word wasn't in Henry's vocabulary. When I first met him, he had recently lost his wife of many years, and I could tell that he truly loved and missed her. He often said that he missed her but that he would see her again in heaven. Henry served in the infantry during World War II and was given two Purple Heart medals for being wounded twice. He said he fought against Germans in Europe but had nothing against them since he had just been doing his duty. Henry used hearing aids but they didn't help him much, and you had to practically yell in his ear for him to understand you. He contributed his hearing loss to the war and always called me "Mr. Craig." I liked the sound of it, so I never corrected him about it.

Henry was crying one day and I asked him what was wrong. He said he had a dream about memories of the war the night before. I asked him if he would feel better if he talked about it, and he shared his experiences with me that day although he never spoke of them again. He told me that he had been on patrol one day when someone started yelling his name. It turned out to be his cousin and after warmly greeting one another, they started walking down the street of a town which the Americans had taken. His cousin was only a few feet away from him when a mortar hit, and after the smoke cleared, Henry looked over to see there was nothing left of him.

Henry was first wounded while walking down the road

leaving the town. The treetops had started exploding and he had run toward a barn but hadn't quite made it. He remembered being hit in the leg by something that felt like fire and passing out. He was later patched up and sent back to the front lines.

Henry cried the most when he told me the story of how he was wounded the second time. He said, "You know something, Mr. Craig, I killed someone!" He was so emotional that I cried with him. He said a German soldier had pinned him down in a grassy field, and neither of them would raise their heads. Finally the German started to fire his rifle after what seemed like hours, and he rose up and aimed his own rifle at the man's head. Henry said that he could see the soldier's worried eyes as they fired simultaneously. The German fell backward and Henry's M-1 rifle was shot out of his hands along with the end of his right thumb. Henry said he didn't stick around, but he knew that he had taken a life.

Even after we left the job I kept in contact with Henry. He told me later that he had cancer, and I asked him if he feared death. He said, "No way." Henry had a grade school education and would quite often ask me questions about things he didn't understand from Sunday school. God created quite a man when he created Henry. I loved that man and I will miss him.

I hope 1 John 4:15-21 will help you understand the kind of man that Henry really was.

If anyone acknowledges that Jesus is the Son of God, God lives in him and he in God. And so we know and rely on the love God has for us. God is love. Whoever lives in love lives in God, and God in him. In this way, God is made complete among us so that we will have confidence on the Day of Judgment, because in this world we are like him. There is no fear in love. But perfect love drives out fear, because fear has to do with punishment. The one who fears is not made perfect in love. We love because he first loved us. If anyone says, 'I love God,' yet hates his brother, he is a liar. For anyone who does not love his brother, whom he has seen, cannot love God, whom he has not seen. And he has given us this command: Whoever loves God must also love his brother.

All of us are God's children, and we need to stop fighting each other and end the stereotyping.

Adolph Hitler tried to develop a master race, but his plan failed. There can only be one master, and that's our God. Philippians 2:5-7 tells us this:

Your attitude should be the same as that of Christ Jesus: Who, being in very nature God, did not consider equality with God something to be grasped, but made himself nothing, taking the very nature of a servant, being made in human likeness.

There is a lot of talk in the news lately about hate groups, but they're nothing new. There have been hate groups like the Nazis and the Klu Klux Klan since the dawn of time, but we must forgive them if they wrong us. Proverbs 10:12 says, "Hatred stirs up dissension, but love covers over all wrongs." Jesus sums it up by saying,

This is the verdict: Light has come into the world, but men loved darkness instead of light because their deeds were evil. Everyone who does evil hates the light, and will not come into the light for fear that his deeds will be exposed. But whoever lives by the truth comes into the light, so that it may be seen plainly that what he has done has been done through God (John 3:19-21).

Stereotypes don't always hold true, and I'll give you an example. One of our friends returned from a trip to Israel and told us that her tour guide was Jewish and the bus driver was Muslim. She said they got along well with each other and when she asked the guide how their relationship with each other was, he responded by saying, "We love each other!" 1 Samuel 16:7 says, "The Lord does not look at the things man looks at. Man looks at the outward appearance, but the Lord looks at the heart."

We installed a birdfeeder in our rock garden recently, and it's a beautiful sight to watch. I noticed something about those birds one day that impressed me. There were all types of birds eating together, and the birds on the ground would wait until the others had eaten before they flew up there to get their meal. The Holy Spirit whispered Psalm 133:1 in my ear. That scripture says, "How good and pleasant it is when brothers live together in unity!"

I tip my hat to the person who developed the Special Olympics and to all those who volunteer to make it the success it truly is. I really feel like that event helped to change the stereotyping of individuals with Down's syndrome. Romans 12:16 says "Live in harmony with one another. Do not be proud, but be willing to associate with people of low position. Do not be conceited."

A friend of ours who taught for years calls these children her "Special Kids." I noticed that a young man with Down's syndrome would come to her house on Saturdays, and she would pay him to do yard work. She told us that special people aren't lazy, it's just that they need a lot of love and guidance.

It's dangerous for anyone to think that people with those challenges are a mistake. Revelation 4:11 says, "God created all things, and by his will they were created and have their being." Don't ever underestimate their capabilities. They have a mind, soul, and spirit just as we do. God loves them as much as He does us. If you know someone with Down's syndrome, show them love and respect because that's what they want. Remember this thought: "To the world you might be one person, but to one person you might be the world!"

Don't ever think the world isn't watching you, because it is. You also need to realize that God's watching you. Listen to what Jesus had to say in Matthew 5:13-16:

> *You are the salt of the earth. But if the salt loses its saltiness, how can it be made salty again? It is no longer good for anything, except to be thrown out and trampled by men. You are the light of the world. A city on a hill cannot be hidden. Neither do people light a lamp and put it under a bowl. Instead they put it on its stand, and it gives light to everyone in the house. In the same way, let your light shine before men, that they may see your good deeds and praise your Father in heaven.*

Have you ever thought about how someone might deliver your eulogy at your funeral? I have, and I hope it reads "He loved the Lord and His people." Jesus said this in Matthew 16:26: "What good will it be for a man if he gains the whole world, yet forfeits his soul? Or what can a man give in exchange for his soul?"

While traveling to Virginia Beach last year, we stopped at a truck stop, and a T-shirt caught my eye. It said, "The cross. It's not about jewelry. It's about Jesus." I thought about creation during that whole week's vacation. We were really down on our luck at the time and God helped me to change my outlook and view of things. I began to see God in all creation and to appreciate the beauty of nature and life itself. Let the waves sweep over your bare feet while walking down the beach at night under a full moon with the one you love, and you'll understand God's creative nature. That got my attention and I wanted to see what His Word had to say about it.

Habakkuk 2:14 says, "For the earth will be filled with the knowledge of the glory of the Lord, as the waters cover the sea." Romans 1:20 tells us, "For since the creation of the world God's invisible qualities—his eternal power and divine nature—have been clearly seen, being understood from what has been made, so that men are without excuse." Genesis 1:1 says, "In the beginning God created the heavens and the earth." After he was finished with all that, He created us.

There's no excuse for denying the existence of God or His Son Jesus. We need to be quite aware of the times that the world is experiencing, because Jesus can return for His people anytime.

I was sitting in the park the other day when I noticed a man walking across a field. I noticed that the farther he walked away from me, the smaller he appeared. People that walked toward me would appear to get larger. My question to you is, "Does Jesus appear to be getting larger or smaller to you?" I'll leave you with this. Stop viewing the world with your natural eyes and start viewing it through spiritual ones.

CHAPTER SIXTEEN

Cover-up!

It's common practice to cover the framing members of a home, and since I know of no one who desires to live in a home that has exposed studs and joists, it's time to cover them up. This chapter will explore what you're covering your problems up with and help you understand why you continue to cover up your past.

So let's roll up our sleeves and get started. Before the interior wall and ceiling finish is applied, insulation needs to be in place. The wiring, plumbing, ductwork, and other utilities will need to be roughed in too.

Although there are several types of interior finishes, lath and plaster was most widely used in the past. However, the use of drywall materials has dramatically changed all that. Many builders select drywall because it saves time. A plaster finish requires drying time before other interior work can be started, whereas drywall does not. Drywall is a thin, lightweight board noted for its fast installation and low cost, and is used in the majority of new residential and commercial buildings. Gypsum board is a sheet material made up of gypsum filler faced with paper. These sheets are normally 4' wide and 8' long, but may be obtained in lengths up to 16'. The edges along the length are tapered, allowing for a filled and taped joint.

Now let's talk about covering up mistakes. If you're the type of person who thinks you never make a mistake, you're in for a rude awakening. The only person who ever lived and walked on this earth free of mistakes was Jesus. The simple point I'm trying to make is that we all make mistakes and gain nothing by trying to cover them up.

We have the divine promise from our Savior that we can be forgiven of our sins, no matter what they may be. When we realize our shortcomings, we need to immediately ask our Lord for forgiveness. You cannot hide a spiritual defect from the Father, and trying to bury past sin without obtaining forgiveness will only make matters worse. We all fall short, and I guess we were designed that way by the Father for a reason. Cleanse your soul and cleanse it often by simply saying something like, "Forgive me, Lord, I made a mistake. I blew it!"

My wife and I recently caught our youngest daughter Katie in a lie and grounded her. I tucked her into bed that night and I can remember telling her this: "You made a mistake by lying, kiddo. You not only have to ask your parents to forgive you, but you have to ask Jesus to forgive you too." She said nothing while I slowly closed the door.

The next morning Katie told me that she had become so overwrought with the thought of committing that sin that she lay in her bed crying for over an hour after I left the room. After wrestling with the Holy Spirit and her emotions, she finally said, "I messed up, Lord, I'm sorry." She said a warm feeling drifted over her, and she finally went to sleep.

Admitting Mistakes

We were building a new home in a subdivision located near Indianapolis. The carpet had just been laid and it looked nice, but the doors rubbed. That happens from time to time but it's easily fixed. In those cases, we remove the doors from the frames and trim off the bottoms. We had to trim roughly a half-inch off and the best way to do it was on the table saw. I assigned Katie to help me with it.

We trimmed a couple of doors and leaned them against the wall, but while we were cutting the third door Katie forgot to hold the strip that was being cut. The rotation of the blade threw it right past my head and it stuck in one of the doors that were leaning against the wall. I stood up, looked at the door, and then pulled the projectile out of it.

After I examined the rather large hole, I stared at Katie. She had a sheepish look on her face and said, "Sorry! Boy, we sure got some major coverin' up to do on that one, dude!" I couldn't stay mad at her for very long after that funny comment, so I laughed it off and repaired the door. I also told the homeowner of the mistake, of course.

It's not our practice to lie about mistakes and cover them up. I'm always honest with customers and I tell them that if we make a mistake we'll fix it. Philippians 4:8 says, "Whatever is true, whatever is noble, whatever is right, whatever is pure, whatever is lovely, whatever is admirable—if anything is excellent or praiseworthy—think about such things."

If you happen to make a mistake, just admit it. Then try to make it right. If you try to cover up the mistake with a lie, you've committed two sins. You've made a mistake and you've lied about it. It's always possible that no one will ever find out about the mistake you made or the lie you told, but you will never be able to hide that from the Lord. Repent and don't do it again.

If it will help, just think of your boss as you do your heavenly Father. You're supposed to listen to your boss and obey his or her instructions. It's also a bad idea to lie to the boss because it can get you fired. Most bosses will understand if you make a mistake, and they'll probably say "Just try not to make that same mistake again." Your earthly boss will give you a second chance and so will your heavenly One. God actually gives us more chances than we really deserve.

Lying will get you in trouble every time. Jesus hates lies, and He said Satan was the father of lies because there is no truth in him. Jesus said that when Satan lies, he speaks his native language. He hates the truth and twists it into a lie to serve his evil purpose. Now's a good time to give you the opportunity for Bible study. If you have a burning desire for the truth and want to know where Jesus talks about liars, it's found in the book of John.

Some lawyers make a career out of twisting the truth and will do anything to win their case in court. I've even seen witnesses lie on the stand in court several times. It's my opinion that most people don't have a problem with lying, even after they place their hand on the Bible and swear to tell the truth, the whole truth, and nothing but the truth, so help them God. It's a good thing that we have Bibles in the courtrooms, but it would be even better if the judges and lawyers were to pick them up and start reading them.

In the movie "Liar, Liar," Jim Carrey plays a lawyer who doesn't tell the truth. One day, his young son is granted a birthday wish that his dad won't lie for 24 hours. Jim Carrey's character can't lie during that time and in the end he says, "This truth stuff is pretty cool!" Believe me, it's not cool to lie. Leviticus 19:11 says not to lie, and Proverbs 19:22 says that "What a man desires is unfailing love; better to be poor than a liar." The footnote for that verse says, "A man's greed is his shame." If you're a liar then you're in the same league as Satan. How can you expect the Lord to continually forgive you over and over and over again for repeated lies? Be careful about telling lies, you might get good at it. If that happens, then you're in for a major fall.

If you have a problem with lying, ask someone to pray with you. You and your prayer partner need to ask the Holy Spirit to deliver you from that obsession. Ask the Holy Spirit to check your lips before a dishonest thought can be vocalized. If you're speaking to someone and you tell a lie, correct yourself immediately. If you're not sure, don't make something up. Just say, "I'm not sure," or "I don't know that to be a fact." It may not be easy to tell the truth at first, but it will get easier. Don't forget to ask Jesus for forgiveness when you do.

We could have hidden the truth about her adoption from our daughter Randie, but we chose not to. Cindy and I did the right thing by not living a life of lies by covering up the adoption. Tell your kids the truth, and they'll really respect you for it. If you decide to lie, you may be able to run from the truth for a while, but you won't be able to hide from it. The truth will find you out. And besides, God is always watching and listening.

We have a satellite dish, and I watch "Court TV" on it from time to time. A few months ago I was watching a New Jersey murder case in which a rabbi was on trial for hiring a hit man to kill his wife of 29 years. It was quite interesting to watch, and it was like something out of a movie, except that it was real. The prosecutor had a tough job to do. He had to convince a panel of 12 jurors that the defendant had forgotten all about Exodus 20:13.

As in all court cases, the defendant must come up with some type of defense. In that case, the defense lawyers chose to discredit the prosecution's case by saying the hit man's testimony was nothing but a pack of lies. The hit man had a history of telling tall tales, and as one of the defense lawyers said, "He couldn't tell what the truth was if it was standing in front of him!"

The prosecution said the rabbi wanted his wife out of the way because he was having an affair with a woman who was a local radio personality. It appeared to me that all of the evidence pointed to the rabbi's guilt since there were several other witnesses who had heard him say he wished she were out of the way. Even if he hadn't committed the crime of murder, he had committed sin. I never heard him say that he was sorry for his sins, nor did I hear him say that he asked the Father for forgiveness of them.

Matthew 15:18,19 says,

> *But the things that come out of the mouth come from the heart, and these make a man 'unclean.' For out of the heart come evil thoughts, murder, adultery, sexual immorality, theft, false testimony, slander.*

That's what Jesus said, but it also sounds like a reporter's description of that rabbi's case. In case you're wondering, the case resulted in a nine to three hung jury, so I would imagine that the case will be retried.

Filling the Void

Life has its ups and downs and is also filled with, "what ifs" and "maybes." We all know about the hurts that life can have, but what hurts are you covering up? Nothing on this earth can match the peace the Lord can bring to your life if you will only hand that hurt over to Him. I once heard a saying that stuck with me. It goes like this: "Let go, and let God!"

There can be many reasons why people do the things that they do. People will blanket their lives with things like work, lies, drinking, drugs, and even eating. I really think they do that to cover a void in their life. Voids in your life can become deep holes in your spirit that only the Father can fill. Will you let Him fill those voids? You've tried everything else, so why not give Him a try?

I have met several people who claimed to be workaholics, and that's a bad thing, in my opinion. Don't suffocate yourself with work. In America our priorities should be God, family, and then work. People in Asia, and especially Japan, have those three priorities reversed, and many of them are dying at an early age because of it. I know that honor means a great deal to those people but they should listen to what Proverbs 21:21 says: "He who pursues righteousness and love finds life, prosperity, and honor."

I love what Paul says in Romans 8: 28.

And we know that in all things God works for the good of those who love him, who have been called according to his purpose.

God can work it out for you, so just trust Him. Step out of the way and let him be the "I AM" in your life! Well, it's time to wrap this chapter up and I can't think of a better ending than what John 8:32 has to say. It simply says, "The truth will set you free!"

CHAPTER SEVENTEEN

Stained Lives!

I have to be honest with you and tell you that I like this chapter the best. Although it discusses painting and staining in the introduction, it's really about the assurance we all have that Jesus can save us from our sins, no matter how bad our past has been.

Wood is often finished without staining, especially if it has a pleasing and characteristic color. When stain is used, however, it often accentuates color differences in the wood surface because of its unequal absorption into different parts of the grain pattern. With hardwoods, such emphasis of the grain is usually desirable, and the best stains for this purpose are dyes dissolved in either water or solvent. The water stains give the most pleasing results, but they also raise the grain of the wood and require an extra sanding operation after the they are dry. The most commonly used stains are the non-grain-raising ones in solvent, which dry quickly.

Paints may be either oil or latex based. Latex based paints and stains are waterborne, and oil-based paints are organic solvent-borne. They are applied to the wood surface and do not penetrate it deeply, but they form a film surface that completely obscures the wood grain. Latex paints are generally easier to use because water is used in the cleanup process. Also, these paints are porous and allow some moisture movement. In comparison, oil-based paints require organic solvents for cleanup and some are resistant to moisture movement. Of all the finishes, paints provide the most protection for wood against surface erosion and offer the widest selection of colors.

New Perspective on Life

This next story I'm about to present is called "A Lake Called Life."

The setting: Indiana Beach, an amusement park.

The location: Lake Shafer in Monticello, Indiana.

The occasion: Cindy Allen's annual company picnic.

Author: The Holy Spirit, as witnessed through the eyes of a humble servant.

Our journey began as just another fun day in the summer sun, but it would become something far different than that, and a new perspective on life would develop as a result.

After lunch, the group decided to take a one-hour trip across the lake on an old-fashioned steam-powered paddleboat, and the Holy Spirit began to speak to the heart and mind of this humble servant. I began to see my surroundings in the spiritual realm.

Although radio and television commercials describe it as "beautiful Lake Shafer," it is far from beautiful, in fact, it's quite dirty. The water is so brown that it feels like we're floating on a large cup of hot chocolate. The shoreline is covered with several expensive homes, although trash and debris are floating on the lake everywhere. It doesn't seem to matter to the people riding in their boats and on their jet-skis because it's almost as though most of them think they're having fun on this "Lake Called Life," but no one dares to drink the water for fear of getting ill.

Our trip ends when we dock at the boardwalk, which extends over the lake. The local attraction catches our eye. Carp by the hundreds are fighting each other for the junk food handouts that the visitors are throwing them. Each fish acts like he is starving to death for the things of this world. Although what he is partaking of isn't good for him, it may kill him, but he indulges in it anyway.

Suddenly, one of the participants tires of the things of this world and decides to swim away from the crowd in search of something new. That lost soul is guided to the shore by a light that illuminates the darkness. Upon reaching his destination, the one who desires a new life finds a kind and gentle stranger waiting. He stands there waiting with open arms and is clothed in pure white. He says, "I love you! Come, I forgive you of your sins." The forgiven one is introduced to his new-found friend and Savior. His name is Jesus.

1 Corinthians 6:9-11 says:

> *Do you not know that the wicked will not inherit the kingdom of God? Do not be deceived: Neither the sexually immoral nor idolaters nor adulterers nor male prostitutes nor homosexual offenders nor thieves nor the greedy nor drunkards nor slanderers nor swindlers will inherit the kingdom of God. And that is what some of you were. But you were washed, you were sanctified, you were justified in the name of the Lord Jesus Christ and by the Spirit of our God.*

Galatians 5:22-25 goes on to say:

> *But the fruit of the Spirit is love, joy, peace, patience, kindness, goodness, faithfulness, gentleness and self-control. Against such things there is no law. Those who belong to Christ Jesus have crucified the sinful nature with its passions and desires. Since we live by the Spirit, let us keep in step with the Spirit.*

I haven't always been in step with the Spirit myself. In my younger days I drank, ran around with women, and smoked cigarettes and pot. I had a lot of stains on my record, but the

Lord forgave me and cleaned me up. No matter how stained your life is, God can turn all that around. If He could do it for me, He can absolutely do it for you.

Having sex outside of marriage isn't what God had in mind when He defined the word "love." Hollywood thinks quite differently than our Lord does, and they don't view sex the way He does. To be quite honest, there's quite a difference between love and lust. If you have a problem with lust, read Leviticus chapter 18. That chapter details the many types of sexual relationships that the Lord opposes.

Remember our bird feeder? Well, those birds that eat from it can be quite messy, and it sometimes looks like they spill more seed on the ground than they eat. I noticed one day that a stalk of corn and a sunflower were growing under the feeder. Depending on your point of view, you might consider those plants weeds. We need to constantly examine our lives and actions. We may do things from time to time and not know why. If we allow the things of this world (which may or may not seem innocent) to take root in our spirit, that's where our trouble begins. What I'm trying to say is that we should make no room in our lives for weeds.

I was once told that "Life is like an onion; you peel off one layer at a time and sometimes you weep." The Holy Spirit desires to peel off the old and install the new.

Tony Orlando recorded a song in the early 1970s called, "Tie A Yellow Ribbon Around The Old Oak Tree." It was based on a true story of a man who served a three-year prison sentence in Georgia in the 1960s for writing bad checks. The man served his time and was released from prison, but before he was released, he wrote his wife a letter. The man told his wife that if she no longer wanted him, he would stay on the bus and forget about their marriage, but if she would forgive him, she was to tie a single yellow ribbon around the oak tree in their front yard.

The man was full of hope and excitement on his way home, so he shared his story with the other passengers on the bus. When they passed his residence, the bus driver stopped and all of the passengers stood and cheered. You see, his wife displayed her message of forgiveness by placing 100 yellow ribbons around that old oak tree. The moral of the story is that love can wipe away the stains of life.

Proverbs 11:7 says, "When a wicked man dies, his hope perishes; all he expected from his power comes to nothing." Freda, a lifelong friend of my mom, had a brother who was about to expire with no hope. Freda was bound and determined that her loved one wouldn't die lost, so she got in her car and drove to the hospital. It was quite some distance away, and she prayed while she was driving. She cried out to the Lord, "Please don't let him die before I get there!"

When she arrived, she found her brother still alive but just barely. A minister had just left the room and her brother said he joked around but never asked if he was right with the Lord. Freda sat on the corner of her brother's hospital bed and led him to the Lord shortly before he passed away. Philippians 1:21 says, "For to me, to live is Christ but to die is gain." Freda's brother gained life that day and God answered her prayers. You see, Freda is much like me. She's had a hard life, but she loves the Lord with all of her heart and she loves her fellow man equally. Freda desires that none be lost, and God is truly pleased with that.

Job 14:14 says that "If a man dies, will he live again? All the days of my hard service I will wait for my renewal to come." Jesus goes on to say in John 11:25 and 26, "I am the resurrection and the life. He who believes in me will live, even though he dies; and whoever lives and believes in me will never die." My uncle Rich never understood those words until he was on his deathbed.

Rich was a long haul trucker for years, and it wasn't unusual for him to be on the road for months at a time because he drove from coast to coast. He was a large, kind man, who had a big heart. He would give you the shirt off his back, but he never gave the Lord an opportunity to wash the stains from his life. All that would change on August 25, 1994, when my uncle would die at the age of 67 of brain cancer.

Mom said Uncle Rich gave his heart to the Lord shortly before he died. I had a dream later that I was standing in my front yard and I crying out to heaven, asking Rich to forgive me for not visiting him before he died. In that dream the skies opened up and his voice spoke the words "It's alright!" I cried every time I thought of that dream for weeks.

Jesus can save you from your sins no matter how tarnished your past has been. He's a master at removing spots and stains. Matthew 1:21 says, "She will give birth to a son, and you are to give him the name Jesus, because he will save his people from their sins." 1 Timothy 1:15-16 says,

> *Here is a trustworthy saying that deserves full acceptance: Christ Jesus came into the world to save sinners—of whom I am the worst. But for that very reason I was shown mercy so that in me, the worst of sinners, Christ Jesus might display his unlimited patience as an example for those who would believe on him and receive eternal life.*

The bottom line is that Jesus can cover the stains of our lives with one coat, and He coats them with His blood.

Now that we're pretty close to finishing this project, don't you think it would be a good idea to walk around the neighborhood and introduce yourself to the neighbors? That is a good idea even if you aren't building a home. It's an opportunity to share your faith with others. Some may accept you and others won't, but they will know where you stand with your convictions. Your neighbors will know that a light shines at your house, and when trouble comes their way, they will know who they can lean on.

Customers sometimes get in financial trouble because they simply get in over their heads. It's usually at about this stage when we start seeing the signs of their lack of financial wisdom. If you're seriously thinking about building a home, pray about it first, ask a lot of questions, and most importantly, lean on the Lord for understanding and wisdom. He'll listen.

CHAPTER 18

Getting Connected

An important step in building a house is connecting the water and sewer lines to the house. If you are building close to a municipal utility, you are required to connect to their lines and have no choice in the matter. That particular utility will charge a monthly service fee for your water and sewage. Your water bill is determined by consumption, but so is your sewage bill. The sewage bill is almost always determined by the amount of water you use. If you're not required to connect to a municipal utility, you will have to drill your own private well and install your own private septic system. You are required to obtain a permit for the well and the septic system from the county department of health.

Unless you have the proper equipment, it would be wise to hire a well driller to do this job. They have the general knowledge of where the water is and are required to send information about your well to the state board of health and the county. When you obtain the permit, the county health official will determine the tank size of your septic system and also the size of the distribution field.

Equipping the House

Now it's time to go shopping and pick out some cabinets. There are three basic ways in which cabinets can be obtained. A cabinetmaker may build the cabinets on the job site, piece by piece, from the plans supplied by an architect. The second method is to purchase knocked-down cabinets, which have been produced in a mill. The parts are assembled at the job site and the cabinets are installed as a unit. The third method is to purchase pre-built cabinets that have been mass-produced at a factory.

While we're at it, let's shop for some appliances for that beautiful new kitchen. Because everybody likes to save money, your best bet would be to look for energy efficient ones. Are you the type of person who likes fancy gadgets? Do you like all the bells and whistles, or are you satisfied with the simpler things of life? I'm asking you, in a roundabout way, if you're proud or humble. I used to be full of pride, but God is changing all that.

When you're talking about furnishing a home, you can buy the basics or you can go all out. I guess you might say that the basics are electricity, water, a phone, and a television. On the other end of the spectrum, you have things like whole home vacuum systems, intercom systems, elaborate security systems, phones in every room, televisions in every room, computers in every room, and a connection to the Internet. I've heard people say that men like their toys, but I know that women like theirs, too.

I wasn't exaggerating when I said some people have a television set in every room. We have a small black-and-white television set sitting on our kitchen counter. My girls usually can't wash the dishes without watching television. There are even television sets and VCRs that mount on the ceiling of your vehicle so you can be entertained while you're driving down the road. One of my college professors told me once that television was poison and the biggest waste of time that was ever invented, and I'm beginning to think she's right!

I've always wanted to ask this question. Would Jesus buy

tickets to an R movie, get a bag of popcorn and a coke, and sit down and watch it?" I don't think so. When you allow that sort of thing in your home or you entertain yourself with it, you are polluting your mind and spirit.

I can barely watch the news on CNN or the networks anymore because it's so depressing. I came across a scripture in James that I believe speaks volumes about the mindset and vocabulary of many of those who produce the television shows, movies, and even the news that we watch. "No man can tame the tongue. It is a restless evil, full of deadly poison" (James 3:8).

Television became a real problem for us, and it got to the point that watching it was all we were doing. We were watching things that simply weren't godly. I finally realized that and began to control our viewing before it controlled us. I'm not saying that everyone's family has a problem with television, but most people really do. I can tell you without a doubt that Jesus and His Father don't approve of most of the things that are shown on it. If you have a problem with television as we did, control it before it controls you.

The meat and potatoes of this chapter is simply this: Americans think they always need to be entertained and that's quite a phenomenon. I saw on the news the other day that a church in Indiana built a Starbuck's coffee shop in the lobby. The pastor was bragging about its success because it was one of a kind, but other pastors who were interviewed for that story didn't share the same feelings that he did. The reporter made the statement that it's a groundbreaking time for the church because they're going where no one else has gone before.

There's a church being built in Texas that will have a McDonalds restaurant inside its walls. Do you know why Americans love to be entertained, and why they desire to eat a Big Mac during the sermon? It's because they desire the things of the world more than they do the things of God. It's a trick of the enemy to get your mind confused and away from God. James 1:19-21 says,

My dear brothers, take note of this: Everyone should be quick to listen, slow to speak and slow to become angry, for man's anger does not bring about the righteous life that God desires. Therefore, get rid of all moral filth and the evil that is so prevalent and humbly accept the word planted in you, which can save you.

Turn that radio or television off and give God your time. Don't think God's listening? It's time to tune in your spiritual radio and tune out the noise of the world. Don't let the things of this world drown out the voice of God. God wants to come in loud and clear in your life.

The simple fact is that Satan wants to tune out your mind to the things of God. You may think it's innocent to watch those television programs or listen to the lyrics of some songs, but believe me, it isn't. The enemy is setting you up for the kill.

The closer you get to God, the clearer His voice becomes. Before long, the Holy Spirit will be able to whisper in your ear without yelling. It's Satan who loves noise, and it seems like the quiet times are the best times to hear from the Lord. Jesus said this in Matthew 6: 6:

When you pray, go into your room, close the door and pray to your Father, who is unseen. Then your Father, who sees what is done in secret comes to reward you.

My kids turn the radio on as soon as they get in the car. I enjoy driving back and forth from work in silence because that's when I usually talk to God. Sometimes though, I'm impressed to say nothing. There are times when God simply says, "Say nothing, and just bask in my presence." Sometimes it's meaningless to ramble on. The Father knows our thoughts and our needs even before we speak it anyway (Matthew 6:8).

I was driving to work one morning when I asked God something. I can't remember exactly what it was now, but it wasn't anything earth shaking—just something small. God answered that prayer the next day while I was driving to work, and I said, "Why did you do that Lord?"

He answered, "Because you asked."

I became so overcome by that answer that I walked around all day saying, "Because I asked." James 4:2 says, "You have not because you ask not!"

Have you ever been around someone who is a fantastic listener? They talk very little, but when they do say something, it's powerful. That's an excellent description of God, wouldn't you say? Sometimes we think God's not listening, but that simply isn't true. It's just that He's not always talking like we think He should be. He won't answer every single question we have, you know.

If you have a need that some may say is scientifically impossible to fill, remember those words aren't defined in God's holy dictionary. Jeremiah 32:17 says, "Ah, Sovereign Lord, you have made the heavens and the earth by your great power and outstretched arm. Nothing is too hard for you." God's listening, but you must ask and then believe.

I remember a Christmas a number of years ago that was pretty grim. The girls were quite small, Cindy didn't have a job, and I was barely making ends meet by working as a hospital janitor in Indianapolis. I remember that it was Christmas Eve and I had no money for presents or food. We were lucky to have a loaf of bread and a gallon of milk. I remember a faint knock at the door that night. The girls opened the door and yelled, "It's Santa Claus."

A man dressed like Saint Nick walked past me saying, "Ho, Ho, Ho," and placed a large sack of toys on our kitchen table. As soon as he did, the girls yelled, "Dad, look!" It appeared that Santa had a couple helpers. They carried in several grocery sacks full of food. They said they couldn't stay, but they did smile and say, "Merry Christmas!"

I found out later that our welcome friends were from the Lebanon Jaycees, and that they had spent their entire budget of $1,000 on us. To this day, I still don't know how they found out about our plight.

I told my youngest daughter Katie about it, and she was so moved that she wrote the story for her English class when the students were asked to write about their favorite Christmas memory. Believe me, I cried when she read it.

As a final note, I would like to share something with you that I found in one of the local newspapers. It's called, "'Twas The Night Before Jesus Came."

'Twas the night before Jesus came and all through the house, not a creature was praying, not one in the house.

Their Bibles were laid on the shelf without care, in hopes that Jesus would not come there.

The children were dressing to crawl into bed, not once ever kneeling or bowing a head.

And mom in her rocker with babe on her lap was watching the "Late Show" while I took a nap.

When out of the east there arose such a clatter, I sprang to my feet to see what was the matter.

Away to the window I flew like a flash, tore open the shutters and threw up the sash!

When what to my wondering eyes should appear but angels proclaiming that Jesus was here.

With a light like the sun sending forth a bright ray I knew in a moment this must be THE DAY!

The light of his face made me cover my head. It was Jesus! Returning, just like he had said.

And though I possessed worldly wisdom and wealth, I cried when I saw him, in spite of myself.

In the Book of Life, which he held in his hand, was written the name of every saved man.

He spoke not a word as he searched for my name; when he said, "It's not here," my head hung in shame.

The people whose names had been written with love, he gathered to take to his Father above.

With those who were ready he rose without a

sound, while all the rest were left standing around.

I fell to my knees, but it was too late; I had waited too long and thus sealed my fate.

I stood and I cried as they rose out of sight; Oh, if only I had been ready tonight.

In the words of this poem the meaning is clear; the coming of Jesus is drawing near.

There's only one life and when comes the last call, we'll find that the Bible was true after all!"

—*Author Unknwn*

I'll leave you with this final thought: Read, pray and learn. God's listening!

CHAPTER NINETEEN

The Path!

The Lord chose well when He chose the name of this chapter. I find that I'm beginning to cherish the meanings of words. Some are quite powerful. I was curious about the definition of path so I looked it up. It's defined as, "A way beaten, formed, or trodden by the foot of a person. A narrow walk or way. A route, course, or track along which someone moves. A course of action, conduct, or procedure."

There are two chapters in this book that are dedicated to someone or something. Chapter Four was dedicated to fallen loved ones. Shortly after the September 11th tragedy, the Spirit told me to dedicate this chapter to those ministers who feel like giving up.

If you're like many who feel that a minister is one who stands in the pulpit and preaches, you're wrong. Most of us have the misconception that the pastor is the only one who is in charge of the poor, the needy, or the lost. Either we don't care, or we simply don't understand what our involvement should be in the work of the Father. We're all called to be ministers. You don't have to go to Bible College or have a certificate, or degree. No one in the Bible did, but God used them anyway because they wanted to make a difference.

I thought about listing all the people who could be ministers, but the list would simply be too long to write. If I listed all the job descriptions that exist, the pages would look like an encyclopedia. What I'm saying is that if you're a Christian, you're a minister, period. It doesn't matter if your official title is "pastor" or not.

God has chosen your path just as He's chosen mine. Listen to what the Spirit has to say in these pages. God really does love you; He cares, and so do I.

Before we begin our construction topic of discussion I'd like for you to listen to the encouragement of Proverbs 4:10-23.

Listen, my son, accept what I say, and the years of your life will be many. I guide you in the way of wisdom and lead you along straight paths. When you walk, your steps will not be hampered; when you run, you will not stumble. Hold on to instruction, do not let it go; guard it well, for it is your life. Do not set foot on the path of the wicked or walk in the way of evil men. Avoid it, do not travel on it; turn from it and go on your way. For they cannot sleep till they do evil; they are robbed of slumber till they make someone fall. They eat the bread of wickedness and drink the wine of violence. The path of the righteous is like the first gleam of dawn, shining ever brighter till the full light of day. But the way of the wicked is like deep darkness; they do not know what makes them stumble. My son, pay attention to what I say; listen closely to my words. Do not let them out of your sight, keep them within your heart; for they are life to those who find them and health to a man's whole body. Above all else, guard your heart, for it is the wellspring of life.

I'm praying that you haven't chosen the wrong path yet, but since life doesn't stand still, neither should we. We have to construct a path to our new home. Those paths are called sidewalks and driveways.

Driveways and walks should be installed before you plant shrubs and trees, or seed and sod the lawn areas. Concrete and pavement are most commonly used in the construction of walks and drives, especially in areas where snow removal is important. In some areas of the country, a gravel driveway and a flagstone or precast concrete walk may be satisfactory, thereby reducing your cost.

Childhood Innocence

Let's talk about the path of a child. I'd like to tell you a humorous story about one's childhood innocence. The Bible tells us that we need to have the faith of a child, and I believe we also need the mind of a child. Children have an innocent mind and the behavior that goes along with it. It was Randie's first day of school, and I had just given her sister a bath and laid her down for a nap. We have a fairly long driveway and I walked with Randie to wait for the bus. Randie and I were waiting at the end of the drive when the bus pulled up, and the kids on the bus were hanging out the windows laughing, and even the driver was cracking up. I looked at Randie and she looked at me. We were puzzled and we couldn't figure out what was so funny. I looked at the driver and said, "Fred, what's so funny?" He was laughing so hard that he was crying, so the only thing he could do was point. I turned around to look and instantly became embarrassed. Raine wasn't asleep at all but was walking down the driveway stark naked. She was strolling down the lane with only a set of boots on her feet and an open umbrella resting on her shoulder. I told Randie to get on the bus, scooped Raine up, and ran back in the house.

To this day, that's Raine's favorite story. I shared it with you, not only to give you a good chuckle, but also to make a point about childlike innocence. Raine never thought about being naked until I told her she was. Although she was a child, Raine was showing the simplicity or naiveté of an unworldly person. Who says we can't learn from kids?

Choosing God's Way

When my wife and I were first dating we decided to take a trip to Cumberland Falls in Kentucky. We decided to go hiking, but we weren't very smart about it. Instead of sticking to the path we decided to make our own trail, like many of us unfortunately do. That was a big mistake, and we became totally lost and wound up down by the river, surrounded by giant boulders. Our only way of escape was to climb those boulders, and though it was quite dangerous, we made it.

Do me a favor and choose God's path. It may have an obstacle here and there along the way, but if you let the Spirit be your guide you'll never become deceived or lost. Matthew 22:14 says, "For many are invited, but few are chosen." I didn't really think about it before, but God has chosen us because we have chosen Him. The road to heaven is narrow and most of the time quite rough, but the highway to hell is wide and very smooth.

Listen closely to how Jesus describes our choice of paths in Matthew 7:13-14.

> *Enter through the narrow gate. For wide is the gate and broad is the road that leads to destruction, and many enter through it. But small is the gate and narrow the road that leads to life, and only a few find it.*

That happens to describe a lot of people. Take rock and roll stars, for example. The group AC/DC wrote a song called "Highway to Hell." I've always said to be careful about what you say and what you ask for, because you just might get your wish. Shortly after that song came out, the lead singer of the group got his wish. He got drunk one night, passed out, and drowned in his own vomit. Several other famous rock stars have died that way, and it's not an elegant way to die. The largest majority of them died at an early age. That's how Satan rewards his followers.

Now do you see what Paul was talking about in 2 Corinthians 11:14 when he said Satan masquerades himself as an angel of light? He decorates his path with the things of the world that look good but are deadly to eat. That path may look good, but as I said before, it's full of "booby-traps" that will kill you.

I was wondering why Jesus spoke in parables one day when the Bible fell open to Mark 4:9-12. If Jesus tried to explain the higher realm to us, we'd have a difficult time understanding it, so He used parables to help us relate. I want you to listen closely to this parable about paths. It's located in Mark 4:14-20:

> *The farmer sows the word. Some people are like seed along the path, where the word is sown. As soon as they hear it, Satan comes and takes away the word that was sown in them. Others, like seed sown on rocky places, hear the word and at once receive it with joy. But since they have no root, they last only a short time. When trouble or persecution comes because of the word, they quickly fall away. Still others, like seed sown among thorns, hear the word; but the worries of this life, the deceitfulness of wealth and the desires for other things come in and choke the word, making it unfruitful. Others, like seed sown on good soil, hear the word, accept it, and produce a crop - thirty, sixty or even a hundred times what was sown.*

I don't know a lot about Enoch, but it's my desire to be like him. Genesis 5: 24 says that "Enoch walked with God; then he was no more, because God took him away." That's my kind of path! I interpret that scripture to mean that Enoch didn't die, but that God simply took him. Other scriptures say that the other people around him died, but it doesn't say that about Enoch. That's the type of intimacy the Lord desires to have with us.

If you decide to change your direction, Satan may try to block the path. He tried to block mine with colon cancer before I started writing this book, but guess what? It didn't work! This book is full of stories about walking in the Spirit and walking down the path of life. Satan will leave you alone if you so desire to choose his path, but if you decide to play it God's way, he may try to kill you. Just remember that Satan can do only what God allows.

Listen pastor, the anointing is your path, and without it the service is just another social event. I know you may be discouraged and want to quit. It may look like the heart of the people has grown cold. Believe me, the winds of change are coming. Pray for the anointing of the Holy Spirit. Pray for it upon your people and yourself. Pray this: "Holy spirit, I pray that your convicting power will continually rest upon this place. I pray that it will be so strong that your people will either enter in or run for the exits."

Pastor, I don't want you to respond by quitting. You're up to bat and the bases are loaded. It's the ninth inning and there's a three ball and two strike count on the world. Satan's trying to convince you to throw down the sword of truth and walk away. If you do that, he'll throw a heater right down the middle for a strike. He'll win, and those you love but who are not saved will lose. The Spirit is standing in the batter's box with you, and he says, "Swing for the fence!" If you stay in there, Satan knows he'll lose the game, so the only way he can win is by deception. If you don't swing at life, we'll all lose. God says, "Stick around and see how the game ends. Don't miss the celebration afterwards, the celebration of my Son's return!"

Jesus said, "Let your light shine before men" in Matthew 5:16. It may not seem like your light is shining on the face of the people now, but that's going to change. Revival will start in their hearts, and believe me, the anointing is the key. You may be a great people person or an excellent teacher, but if there's no anointing, it's futile. The words you speak will just be words. They will float around in the air aimlessly until the anointing of the Holy Spirit becomes present. He will grab those words and pierce the heart of His people with their truth.

I honestly desire the best for each and every one of you,

and it's my sincere prayer that you change your mind if you're thinking about quitting.

I'll leave you with this: "Following the path of least resistance is what makes rivers and men crooked!"

CHAPTER TWENTY

Was It Worth It?

We're in the process of applying the finishing touches to everything. Because building a home is such a vast project, it requires roughly three or four months to complete, not to mention the great expense. At the end, though, we can sit back and enjoy the accomplishment. I almost always ask the customer if they're satisfied with the work, but I also ask, "Was it worth it?"

A great number of contractors will do what's called a "walk-through." A walk-through is an inspection when the contractor and customer walk through the home with the intention of looking it over with a "fine-toothed comb." After the walk-through is complete, the contractor will have the customer sign-off on it. If there are defects that still need to be corrected, a customer should never sign-off on the project.

We just completed another year, and I'm quite amazed by the things going on around us. I'm also quite humbled by God's presence. I don't regret the past because I knew that the Lord was with me every step of the way, and I don't fear the future either. It's my sincere prayer that you will draw closer to the Lord more than you ever have done before. I pray that you will develop a hunger and a thirst for Him like you've never experienced before. When you get to that stage of your life, God is quite pleased. I don't know about you, but I'm starving to death for the things of God.

I'm astonished by the chapter names that the Lord picked out in this book, and I especially marvel at this one. How many times have you posed the question, "Was it worth it?"

I used to think that I was on top of the world and could handle anything. I was a fool, and I was wrong. I finally realized that God was the Lord of my life, and that I was His servant. That's where most of us get into trouble. We want to be the boss and not the servant. That's where the struggle begins. It's a struggle against good or evil. I choose to struggle against evil, how about you?

It was the middle of December last year and we were getting ready to go to Sunday school, but I really didn't feel good. I had been experiencing a dull pain in my right rib cage area for a couple of weeks, but like most men, I thought the pain wasn't that bad and that it was something that I could live with. I thought, "I'm just getting older and there's no need to go to the doctor," but it wouldn't take long for me to find out that my line of thinking was in error.

We arrived at church that morning and it was a pleasant service, but throughout it the pain started to intensify. Because our church is such a large one, prayer teams have become a tradition. Traditions can be good and then they can be bad. A prayer team consists of two individuals who stand at the altar, and the pastor will invite anyone who desires prayer to stand in line. Those in line are led to the prayer teams.

I got in line that morning and I was prayed for. I appreciated it, but that young couple wasn't prepared for their task that day. The anointing simply wasn't there, and although their intentions were good, I didn't get any better. In fact, I got worse.

Right before the service ended, I began to think I'd better see my doctor on Monday, but the Holy Spirit immediately interrupted my train of thought. He said, "Don't wait until tomorrow. Go to the emergency room today!" I told Cindy what the Spirit had said and she agreed, but asked if I could stand to get a bite to eat before we went.

We decided to visit Taco Bell, and we paid for our food and started to sit down. An excruciating pain shot through my right side when I tried to sit down, and it was so great that it was all I could do to hold back the tears. That attack lasted for only a few seconds, but it felt like an eternity. We finished our meal and as I was climbing into the car, another attack occurred.

We drove straight to the hospital, and after we registered, the doctor examined me. He asked me a large number of questions and one of them was, "Have you had blood clots before?"

When I said yes, he said, "That's it." He then looked at me and said, "Got any extra clothes with you?"

I said, "No, why?"

"Because I'm admitting you, you're not going anywhere!" He then went on to say that these things are serious matters, and that they can kill you. I remained in the hospital for roughly three days while they conducted a series of tests on me. My family doctor paid me a visit and sat at the end of my bed and told me that the tests had ruled out blood clots.

I said, "Thank God for that!"

He said, "Not so fast, you've got another problem."

He began to describe my condition. He told me I had "pleurisy," which can be quite nasty and painful. He tried to tell me the medical term for my condition, but even he had a hard time pronouncing it.

After prescribing medication, my doctor decided to let me go home the next day. I had a few visitors that night but it was a relatively quiet evening until the time for lights out came. Shortly before I fell asleep I had a vision. In the vision I saw Satan jab his long bony finger in my side, and I knew that was my answer. That was why I was in there.

I eventually drifted off to sleep, but soon felt something choking me. Three nurses awakened me. They kept saying, "Mr. Allen, Mr. Allen."

I looked at them and said, "What do you need?"

All three of them looked at me and said, "You flat-lined!"

One of the nurses said, "He's probably just pulled one of the wires off his remote heart monitor. I don't see any loose wires though."

Another nurse spoke up and said, "Even if that's the case, his heart rate dropped down to 38 last night."

I looked at her and asked, "What's it supposed to be?"

She told me that it's supposed to be around 80 or 90. She also said that I had given them quite a scare and that the doctor wasn't letting me go until I had a stress test done.

The technician picked me up for the test at about noon on Wednesday. I called home that morning and mentioned that I had flat-lined. That really scared Randie, and she decided to call our church. The pastor was busy, so she talked to one of the assistant pastors.

At the precise time the technician arrived in my room, the assistant pastor called. He asked to pray for me over the phone and I said, "Absolutely!" I didn't find out until much later, but my mom was praying the exact same prayer across town when the assistant pastor called. Their prayers were virtually identical! They prayed that the tests would result in nothing, and they did.

While I was in that hospital I told the Lord that I was going to make the time count for Him. On the first day I told one of the nurse's aides that I was writing this book, and she asked what it was about. I told her that it was full of miraculous stories, and she said, "Tell me one." So I told her the angel story.

When I arrived at the department that conducted the stress test, I found two female employees, one male employee, and a doctor. It was around Christmas time and they were listening to Christmas CDs. The conversation started when the doctor asked me what I thought of Amy Grant. I told him I thought she was leaning on the things of the world, and the conversation turned to Christianity. I asked the doctor if he was a Christian and he told me he was. I told him I was writing this book, and he began to share his thoughts with me. It was quite an amazing sight, actually. I was sitting there with wires all over me and the doctor was standing above me asking questions about Christ. The employees were standing in silence around us while the doctor and I carried on our conversation about our faith. The doctor told me that he was going to do something starting in 2002 that he had never done before. He was going on mission trips.

I said, "God's going to bless you for that."

He told me when the book comes out he wants me to deliver him a signed copy. I will most certainly do that.

When I was ready to leave, I overheard the male employee talking on the phone to another employee who had called in sick that day. He was telling her all about my book and how wonderful it was going to be.

I want to emphasize the point that God always finishes what He starts, and that we are the ones who fall short and desire to quit. I think I mentioned it before but it's worth mentioning again: If you don't have a personal journal you should start one. It will make it much easier to remember the things that God is doing in your life.

Do you ever feel like life is a fight and Satan's taken his gloves off? Well, you're not alone. I feel the same way. But it's not all your fight, you know. Jesus is in your corner. Listen to what the following scriptures have to say about fighting:

"Fight the good fight of faith" (1 Timothy 6:12).

"The Lord will fight for you; you need only to be still" (Exodus 14:14).

"Do not be afraid of them, the Lord your God himself will fight for you" (Deuteronomy 3:22).

"Wherever you hear the sound of the trumpet, join us there. Our God will fight for us" (Nehemiah 4:20)!

"For our struggle is not against flesh and blood, but against the rulers, against the authorities, against the powers of this dark world and against the spiritual forces of evil in the heavenly realms" (Ephesians 6:12).

Is the call to arms ringing in your ears yet?

I attended church with a Christian brother who learned that man can be remodeled, literally, by the fire. When Randy's house burnt, he approached us about getting an estimate to repair the damages. I thought, "Thank God he's got insurance." We would find out later that his insurance company cared more about their profits than they did his well-being. It would be his first and last claim with that company.

I met Randy at the house and surveyed the damage with him. He said everybody had gotten out when the fire started. He'd grabbed a garden hose from his brother, who lived next door, and tried to put out the fire. He'd broken out the front window and sprayed water on the flames, but it had become quite obvious that the fire was getting out of control, so he yelled, "Call 911!" The fire department arrived and extinguished the fire relatively quickly. Thank God nobody got hurt, but it's only by the grace of God that I can say that.

The fire had started in the front bedroom and had damaged the downstairs front bedroom, living room, and the entire second floor. I found an exposed gas line in the bedroom where the fire started. I looked at Randy and said, "It's only by the grace of God that you and your neighbors are still alive!"

He asked, "Why?"

I told him that the gas line was still active. If that line had exploded, it would have leveled the entire block, and probably killing everyone in its path.

I wrote Randy an estimate and he turned it in to his insurance company. In the mean time he was staying at a hotel. The insurance company was quite nasty with him. They wrote him a single check that was far below the cost of the repairs, and they dropped him like a hot potato. Obviously he was devastated.

I prayed about it and felt led to do the work for the amount of the check. When God speaks, especially when it concerns money, it's hard for some people to obey, but not me. I told Randy not to worry about a thing, and said, "We're going to get you back in your house, and it will be better than it was before." I didn't realize it at the time, but God was planning to remodel a spirit or two while we were at it.

I remember sitting on Randy's front porch one evening after work while he and I enjoyed the stars and a cool drink. I remember telling him this: "We're almost done with your home but God's doing something far greater than that! He's put me in charge of rebuilding your earthly home but He's going to rebuild your spiritual home. I had a dream about you last night and God said, 'Out of the ashes will come beauty!' Randy, God's not only going to restore your home, but He's going to restore your soul!"

Tears of joy began to stream down Randy's face, and to this day, it's impossible for me to hold back the tears when I think about that night. And God wasn't quite finished yet. There was still a soul or two that needed to be remodeled.

It was the last day on the job, and I was the first to arrive at the job-site. I noticed Randy's sister-in-law standing on her front porch next door, and she was crying. I knew her and her husband, so I asked her what was the matter.

She said, "Nothing."

I said, "I know better than that. What is it?"

She said that her husband Jim was having chest pains and he wouldn't go to the hospital.

I asked her, "Do you want me to talk to him?"

"Please," was her response.

Jim was sitting in his recliner, and I could tell by his facial expressions he was in a great deal of pain. I looked at him and said, "Jim, you know what this is. Stop messing around! Do you want me to pray for you?" He nodded. I prayed for him for quite some time. I knelt down in front of him and said, "Remember when you got saved at work, Jim? Well, you've got an enemy now. He hates everybody that stands for Christ. Satan's trying to kill you, my friend, but I love you and care about you. Will you promise me that you'll let your wife take you to the hospital?" He slowly nodded his head and then he burst out in tears. It was like he couldn't hold it back anymore!

Jim let his wife drive him to the emergency room that day, and thank God that he did. Jim underwent triple by-pass heart surgery, and he and his family are doing quite well. Thank you, Lord, for the opportunity to save someone's life. It was worth it!

I was recently asked by a guy at church to help with a terminally ill cancer patient's roof. The man didn't have long to live, and he had an inoperable brain tumor. His roof was in terrible shape, and he simply needed a new one. I volunteered to help and so did Katie. The guy who was coordinating the project asked quite a few people to help, but only a handful showed up. I told him that I didn't want to be pushy but that someone with experience needed to be in charge.

I pulled our trailer full of tools to the job-site. Things were pretty unorganized at first but started running more smoothly when everyone laid their opinions to the side. The day wore on and volunteers started leaving one by one, but a total of six people, including Katie and myself, stayed late to finish the project. The crew had removed all the old roofing and repaired the existing water damage to the sheathing, and we got his entire roof finished before the sun set.

I remember seeing the neighbors taking pictures of us. I guess they did that because they were amazed by our expression of kindness. The man's mom thanked us while we were preparing to leave. She cried out, "Thanks for helping my boy!"

I looked at Katie and said, "God's pleased with our effort today, and we did a good thing. I thank you and God thanks you."

Proverbs 11:30 says, "The fruit of the righteous is a tree of life, and he who wins souls is wise." It was a wise decision to write this book. It's been a lot of work, and it will have taken approximately eight months to complete, but if it helps one person it will be worth every minute. That's how important I think you are and how important God thinks you are.

God said that pastors would use parts of it in their sermons. I consider that an honor. I say, "Go for it pastors! Bless

God's people and teach them! I thank you, and the Father thanks you."

Is it going to be worth it, being a "Builder of the Spirit?" Absolutely!

CHAPTER TWENTY-ONE

My Mansion—Thanks Lord!

If you like chapter titles, you should love this one. During the course of writing this book, I found that many of the construction terms that are used today were used even in biblical times. Even to this day, most would say that the foundation is the most important feature of your dwelling, and it's the most important feature of your spiritual life, too. It would be in your best interest to remember this: "By wisdom a house is built, and through understanding it is established" (Proverbs 24:3).

We're finished with the building. It's time for you to move in, and time for us to move onto the next job. As you might have guessed, this chapter deals with the finished product. Although your home may be a finished product, your life isn't. You will continue to learn until the day you die. God will always be in the process of molding and shaping you into His image. I like to look at it this way: He is the potter and we're the clay. He's constantly trying to mold us and shape us into something of beauty. There will be times when He has to flatten us and begin creating something new, but we should never view that as a bad thing.

When we enter into a contract with a customer, one of the

common questions we ask is, "Do you want a turn-key building?" Turn-key is a common term that's used in construction to describe the finished product. When the contractor asks the homeowner if they want a turn-key building, they're asking if they want them to do all the work.

Finances restrain some homeowners, so it's quite common for a contractor to have to work within the budget of the customer and only do part of the work. Some homeowners are willing to do what's called "sweat equity." In construction, sweat equity simply means that the owner is willing to do some of the work to get the project completed within their given budget.

I've always been willing to let the customer perform sweat equity, and their lending institution usually dictates the dollar limit for the project. Sometimes there's simply not enough money there to complete what needs to be done, so the homeowner is faced with the decision of either canceling the project or performing free labor.

Sweat equity isn't free from complications though. Some homeowners simply don't have the right tools for the job and their rate of completion can be quite slow and troublesome. When a customer doesn't have a phase of the project completed before we're ready, it really messes up our schedule. Another factor to be concerned with is that some homeowners have never done anything like it before and it usually results in poor workmanship. Think hard before you try to tackle sweat equity. The service of the Lord may be sweat equity but it's got great benefits.

Dealing With Pride

Now that you have that new home, how long will it take for pride to set in? There are many who suffer from that debilitating condition called pride. Without Christ it's hard to overcome a spirit of pride. In fact, it's suffocating. Debt and pride usually go hand in hand.

Proverbs 16:5 says, "The Lord detests all the proud of heart. Be sure of this: They will not go unpunished." Proverbs 16:16-19 goes on to say,

How much better to get wisdom than gold, to choose understanding rather than silver! The highway of the upright avoids evil; he who guards his way guards his life. Pride goes before destruction, a haughty spirit before a fall. Better to be lowly in spirit and among the oppressed than to share plunder with the proud.

Proverbs 8:13 says, "To fear the Lord is to hate evil; I hate pride and arrogance, evil behavior and perverse speech."

We should all feel that way. We shouldn't be proud people, but we should be humble. I can assure you that God hates arrogance and pride. When you're a proud person, God usually has His ways of knocking your legs out from underneath you.

I remember the first employee I ever hired when I started business. His name was Joe, and although he was full of pride at first, that soon changed. You see, Joe got saved and gave his heart to Christ. He not only gave the Lord his heart, but he gave him his life. Joe used to live for the things of the world, but he now lives for the things of Christ. He's married to a great lady, they have kids, and he's a minister in the Baltimore, Maryland area. The story ends well and I was glad to be a part of his life.

Ecclesiastes 3:1 and 2 says, "There is a time for everything, and a season for every activity under heaven: A time to be born and a time to die."

The Father has something waiting for you when you die. Some think that God sends people to hell, but that's not the truth. He always gives us a choice, and we can choose to live for Him or we can choose to live for the devil. Satan would have you believe that nothing happens when you die, but believe this: he has a big surprise in store for the naive ones. It's never been God's desire for any to perish in the lake of fire, but that's the consequence of their choice to live a life of sin and separation from Him. If you choose a life of sin, you also choose separation from God. God is a spirit that is of holy origin, and He will not allow the association of sin in His presence.

Jesus died for our sins. He washed away our sins so we could stand in the presence of the heavenly Father. Don't get me wrong, we all make mistakes, but if we ask Jesus for forgiveness, He will give it to us because He has the authority!

You're promised a mansion in heaven just like the one the chapter title suggests, and I'm convinced that they will be custom built by the hand of the Father Himself. If you make it into heaven by the skin of your teeth, you're going to inherit the basic unit. On the other hand, there are certain other rewards to be achieved. The Bible calls them jewels in your crown. What's your choice? Job 14:14 says, "If a man dies, will he live again? All the days of my hard service I will wait for my renewal to come." The time will come. Death is promised to us all, so choose well, my friend.

I feel led to share one of my journal entry dreams with you because I feel it will help some of you who are struggling with uncertainty. You may know God's got something for you but you don't know what it is, or you do know what it is but you're uncertain of the timing. Remember what I said several chapters ago? God's in control and He's got the master set of plans. The only thing we need to do is follow His specifications when it's time to break ground. I know in my spirit that will speak loudly to some of you.

That journal entry was dated December 27, 2001. I dreamt that I was standing in the lobby of a motel, and there was a gentleman standing there with me. I wasn't sure if he was an employee of the motel or not. There was a criminal hiding there and I was trying to catch him, but after about the second or third time of trying to hide he simply walked out and lifted his hands in surrender. Someone called the police, and when they arrived to arrest him, more criminals began to walk out from their hiding places, and they too wanted to surrender.

Then I noticed something peculiar happening between one of the officers and one of the criminals. The officer took one of the shoes from the criminal, who was handcuffed, and stuffed it in his mouth. I asked the man beside me why he did that, and he said it was because he wouldn't shut up, and he was tired of him talking. I thanked the stranger, and the officers said I was free to go.

I walked a few blocks and saw a small house that looked like a cabin. I was curious, so I walked up to the door and knocked. Much to my surprise, my brother answered the door. That home consisted of one room that was large enough for a bed. I walked in, but I knew from the way he acted that he wasn't glad to see me. I noticed that the bed was covered with ashes. I tried to clean them off but he told me to leave them alone. He kept trying to cover the doors and windows with black sheets. He was even trying to cover the opening to the closet with them. It was quite obvious that he didn't like the light.

There was a knock at the door and I opened it. It was the stranger from the motel, and he had a huge tray of fish. They were already dressed-out and placed under plastic and looked fresh. The stranger said, "We'd better put these in the refrigerator before they spoil," and we did just that. My brother started yelling, "Get out, get out!" When I pulled the fish out of the refrigerator I found that they were already prepared. My brother was quite angry, and he covered all the windows and doors and told us to leave.

As I began to walk toward the street, I noticed an older model pickup truck parked by the curb. As I began to walk towards it, I became quite surprised by the actions of the friendly stranger. He was plowing a path to the truck in the front yard with a tiller. I walked over the tilled ground and two of the fish fell from the tray I was carrying onto the dirt. Those two fish immediately transformed into puppies, so I walked to the truck and placed the remaining fish in the front seat, then walked back to get the puppies. The puppies didn't run, but they stayed put and waited for my return. I picked them up and returned to the truck. The stranger stopped what he was doing and asked if he could go along for the ride, and I said, "Sure."

While I was driving, the puppies decided to crawl behind

me. One crawled behind my neck and the other crawled behind my lower back. I thought I may have been hurting them but I wasn't. They were comforting me. We began to drive up the incline of a hill when I saw a red light in the distance. I engaged the clutch and began to apply the brakes, but as soon as I did, the light turned green. When I let the clutch out, the transmission started slipping and I immediately looked in the rearview mirror to see if anybody was behind me. I didn't want to roll backwards into anybody, but there was no one there. I looked at the stranger who had been with me through all this, but he just sat in the passenger seat with a smile on his face and said nothing. We finally got to the top of the hill, and after we crested it, we started to coast down the other side. That's when I woke up.

Some might say that dream was just meant for me, but I don't think so. I think it was meant to be shared with all of us, and I'll tell you why. As Christians, we will always experience parts of that dream, and I think the best way to help you understand it is to explain what certain parts of it mean.

1) The thief is Satan.

2) Police mean authority. If you notice, the thief surrenders to authority.

3) The stranger is a divine presence that is always with us.

4) Remember the shoe? The word says the head of the serpent will be crushed when he strikes our heel (Genesis 3:15).

5) My brother was sleeping in a bed full of ashes. He didn't want to see the light and he couldn't wait to get rid of us. In other words, Christians and the sin of the world don't mix.

6) I'm convinced that the fish meant souls. If you noticed, I didn't do anything to prepare them. They were already prepared. What I'm saying is, there's a tremendous harvest of souls waiting out there, and God's going to bring them to us.

7) Someone is plowing the ground for us, and making the way.

8) The puppies meant comfort. We will always have a comforter.

9) We will make it up and over the hill, but it won't be easy.

10) When we look behind us there will be no one there to stop us. They will have been silenced!

I know beyond a shadow of a doubt that this will speak to the hearts of many of you, and especially those who are struggling with uncertainty. It's powerful and I thank God for sharing it with us.

I'm going to share another dream with you, and I hope it will show you what you're up against. I had this dream before I started my journal, but I recall it as if it happened yesterday. Before I share the dream with you, though, I'd like to share this thought. "If Satan leaves you alone you better beware!" That's what I tell people when they're in a spiritual battle.

I dreamed that I was standing in an entrance between the living room and kitchen of my aunt and uncle's house, and Jesus was standing there with me. I noticed that my aunt and uncle were eating supper, but they had their heads down and they weren't looking at each other or speaking. There was a mist hovering over their heads. It just seemed to float across the ceiling, but neither one of them ever noticed it. I looked at Jesus and asked, "What is that thing, Lord?" He told me it was a spirit of division.

That dream bothered me so badly that I called my uncle the next day. I told him about the dream and what the Spirit had told me shortly before I called. I told him, "The Lord wants you to be a peacemaker and to love your wife, and not just tolerate her." I told my uncle that the Lord was speaking to him and no one else and that the message was meant just for him. I found out later that he had a discussion with my aunt about it. She told me that he was already a peacemaker and she asked if the fog ever touched them in the dream. I said, "No."

She told me that they pray and go to church, and that the Lord will protect them from the fog, but I told her that she was completely missing the point. God was showing her that there was a spirit of division in their house. I told her that she knew what it was and that she and her husband needed to pray it out of there. I asked her, "Why in the world would you want to live with something like that?"

I felt that neither of them understood God's warning, so I prayed it out of their house. A couple of days later, I had another dream about their house. This time I was standing outside, and I saw a hand extend down from heaven. It was as large as their house and it looked as though it was protecting their home. My mom later told me that she noticed a personality change in my uncle. She said that he appeared to be a kinder and gentler man, even more so than he has been in the past.

We may not always understand what the Lord's saying or what He's doing, but we'd better listen. We may not have the luxury of someone to pray for us, so there are times when we simply have to pray for ourselves. We need to stop, watch, and listen.

We need to not only love our neighbors, but also our relatives, no matter how they treat us. That's why we need to pray for them and keep an eye out for their spiritual safety. Satan doesn't have their best interests in mind either, you know. I'm convinced that God doesn't care about money or things, but that He does care about you and me.

When I first started writing this book, God was not only looking out for my spiritual well being, but He was also looking out for the well being of this book. Throughout the entire writing process, God has brought people my way to assure the completion of his book. To be quite honest with you, I didn't have a clue about what I was doing, but I knew God wanted me to write a book. Shortly after I started writing, I got a shot of encouragement. I went to give an estimate in a neighboring town where I discovered another Christian writer. She helped me a lot and said something that was pretty interesting. She asked how many chapters the book would have.

I said, "Twenty-one."

She said, "That's significant!" I couldn't understand why.

She told me that three multiplied by seven equals twenty-one.

That aroused my curiosity because I knew three represented the Trinity, and I also knew that seven signified the day of completion. I discovered Genesis 2:1-3, and took from it an understanding of how creative a God we serve. He was not only creating a book that would touch the lives of thousands, but he was creating something in me that wasn't even there before. He was literally transforming me into a new creature. Absolutely no one that knows me, including my family, would have ever imagined me being a writer. If God can transform this hardhead, He can transform anybody.

I love the chapter titles and the thoughts and scriptures that are contained within them. They're meaningful and quite powerful. We have a refrigerator magnet that says "Philippians 4:13" on it, and I love the truth behind it. It says, "I can do everything through him who gives me strength." God has kept his promise, and He's given me strength through this entire eight-month project and I'm about to finish my task. Thanks Lord. You never fail!

Deuteronomy 6:5-7 says:

> *Love the Lord your God with all your heart and with all your soul and with all your strength. These commandments that I give you today are to be upon your hearts. Impress them on your children. Talk about them when you sit at home and when you walk along the road, when you lie down and when you get up.*

That's excellent advice that I think we can all benefit from.

I can't let this book end without praying for you. "Lord, I pray for each and every reader that picks up these pages, no matter what their circumstances are. Remove pride from their hearts, and build a longing in their spirit for you! Make them a "Builder of the Spirit!" In Jesus' holy name, I pray, Amen.

Psalms 51:10 says, "Create in me a pure heart, O God,

and renew a steadfast spirit within me." It's time to say, "Yes Lord, build that in me!"

For all of you who like to cook I've got a treat for you before I leave. It's called the "Recipe For Life."

1 cup of good thoughts.
1 cup consideration for others.
3 cups well beaten faults.
1 cup of kind deeds.
3 cups forgiveness.

Mix thoroughly and add tears of joy, sorrow, and sympathy for others. Fold in 4 cups prayers and faith to lighten other ingredients and raise the texture to great heights of Christian living. After pouring all this into your daily life, bake well with the heat of human kindness. Serve with a smile.

I know you're probably thinking, "What kind of book is this? How do I describe it to friends?" Folks, it's one of a kind, but I can tell you this: It's your book! I encourage you to mark the pages and highlight the things that speak to your heart. Write notes in it. It's intended to stimulate your mind, and it's going to mean different things to different people because no two people are alike.

When you try to describe it to a friend just tell them how it touched your heart. That's the purpose of it! If you have a hard time witnessing, buy them a book, especially your relatives, because they are usually the hardest ones to reach. They know you the best, and they know your faults, but this book will touch them in a way that you may not be able to. They will read it in the privacy of their home, and during the "quiet-time" of reading it the Holy Spirit can begin to work on their mind and their life.

This book will touch the heart of the reader, no matter what their age is, while entertaining those from all walks of life. I would best describe the book as an inspirational one.

The book isn't like a novel that you can pass on to somebody when you finish it. It's the type of book that needs to be purchased for just one person. So when you buy one, buy it for that person. Write on the inside of the front cover, "I bought this book for you because I love you. Enjoy!" It's an excellent investment in their life and you'll be well on your way to being a builder yourself.

This isn't the only book I'm going to write. I am going to start writing the second one immediately after I finish this one, so keep an eye out for it. It will be called, "The Bored and the Cross." Without giving away the story line, I'll just tell you that it's about a modern day Moses with a backpack.

For quite some time the Spirit had been saying, "The Bored and the Cross," but that's all He was saying. I had a pretty good feeling that He had another book in mind, but other than that I didn't give it much thought. I thought He meant "The Board and the Cross" until one Saturday. I went to pick up the mail that morning and He said, "It's not spelled B-O-A-R-D. It's spelled B-O-R-E-D!"

When I stuck my hand in the mailbox, He instantaneously gave me the entire story line for the book, and I walked around all day in amazement that He could do that. Folks, we don't have a clue what He's capable of, and we don't have a clue what our mind is capable of receiving either.

It's been a lot of fun, but I have to leave you. I leave you with love and these thoughts: Be thankful for what you have, who you are, what God has built, and what he is going to build. I'm handing over the tools to you. Now, it's your turn to be a "BUILDER OF THE SPIRIT!"

For more information, visit our website at
builderofthespirit.com

or drop us a line at
P.O. Box 318
Jamestown, IN 46147